The Private House

The Private House
Rose Tarlow

CLARKSON POTTER/PUBLISHERS

NEW YORK

PUBLISHED BY CLARKSON POTTER/PUBLISHERS, NEW YORK, NEW YORK.
MEMBER OF THE CROWN PUBLISHING GROUP.
RANDOM HOUSE, INC. NEW YORK, TORONTO, LONDON, SYDNEY, AUCKLAND
WWW.RANDOMHOUSE.COM
CLARKSON N. POTTER IS A TRADEMARK AND POTTER AND COLOPHON ARE REGISTERED TRADEMARKS OF RANDOM HOUSE, INC.

PRINTED IN CHINA
DESIGN BY RICHARD FERRETTI

LIBRARY OF CONGRESS CATALOGING-IN-PUBLICATION DATA
TARLOW, ROSE.
      THE PRIVATE HOUSE / BY ROSE TARLOW.—1ST ED.
      1. INTERIOR DECORATION.   I. TITLE.
      NK2110.T27   2001
      747—DC21   00-065586

ISBN 0-609-60472-4
10 9 8 7 6 5 4

For My Father

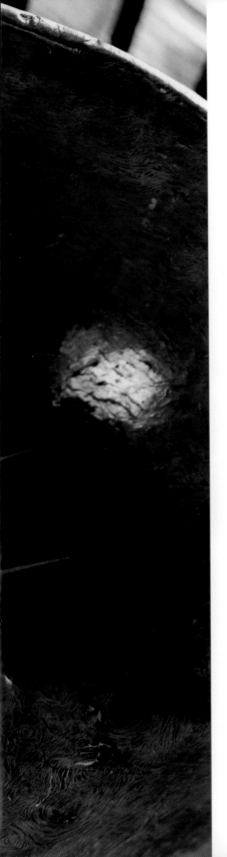

Every designer yearns to create a perfect world; some worlds are more perfect than others. Rose Tarlow's world is made of one part memory and one part physical reality, though a better way of explaining this might be to say that she balances emotion and intellect as well as any designer now living. Emotion is a powerful ingredient in her work—we feel things in her rooms, and when we look at the furniture and fabrics she has designed, they are full of associations that evoke moods and reveries, and yet they are never sentimental. That is where the physical reality comes in. What really controls Rose Tarlow's designs is her eye. She deals in proportion and texture, space and color, and she approaches them as an architect does, with absolute, relentless rigor and a brilliant understanding of how they affect our experience. She is a true connoisseur, in the sense that connoisseurship is, in the end, about knowing. What Rose Tarlow knows is how objects resonate in our minds, and how they come together to shape our feelings. She knows that there are magical things that great objects do, and she knows how to perform the even more elusive magic that consists of juxtaposing objects in ways that become transcendent.

A room full of French furniture set amid paneling brought over whole from a château bores her. Her creative energy is too strong for that. Yet her finest rooms, such as her own living room in Bel Air, which remarkably manages to combine rusticity and dignity, and the serene and glowing library, screening room, and main hall of the enormous house she recently completed in Los Angeles, embody the spirit of classic rooms. They do it, however, through a mix of elements we have never seen before. Every one of them is a complete and whole composition in three dimensions, but to leave it at that makes them seem too much like places only to be looked at. The greatest power Rose Tarlow's rooms have is their ability to make us want to do more than look—they make us want to touch, to sit, to wallow in them.

I do not know how to explain Rose's rooms except to say that they are right. They balance sensual pleasures with geometric rigor, and every one of them is simultaneously a lesson in design and a lesson in living. Her work celebrates the reality of living—the way in which, out of a complex mix of memories, emotions, aspirations, and knowledge, each of us builds a life that is like none other. Rose Tarlow's rooms are like no other, and they are marked by a natural grace.

Paul Goldberger

A Window Inside

PRECEDING PAGE) **An entryway
is an introduction. Like the
opening pages of a book,
it leads us in and welcomes
us to the world inside.**
RIGHT) **The colors from my
paintbox are a never-ending
source of design inspiration.**
OVERLEAF) **An old English
bamboo ladder in a corner
of my living room holds
treasured personal articles.**

I live inside my head, often oblivious to the world outside myself. I see only what I wish to see. Everything else is obliterated by a convenient discerning device, a window inside—a window that, in an instant, will open and record the vision of a single blade of grass reflected in a raindrop, a gift to store in the recesses of my mind. The memory of this moment of pure perfection will be enhanced by the paintbrush of my imagination. This is the source of my creativity.

I have just spent three nights in a dull hotel in Dublin and have no recollection whatsoever of my room. My mind frames only the particular place I need to see, and eliminates any unrewarding details that would cloud my perspective. To this special form of discernment do I owe my successes, and most possibly my shortcomings.

Without a moment's hesitation, I can describe in great detail the aerial view of the unbelievably beautiful quilt of farmland that covers the low, hilly landscape that is Shannon. I am alert, no longer just in my

head. From my airplane window, the clouds are a brilliant translucent white, meshed with so clear and bright a blue that if it were translated onto canvas it would seem totally unnatural. The earth below is blanketed by hundreds of different shades of vivid, glorious green—a kaleidoscope of color that is indelibly etched in my memory. Ireland has provided me with a visual experience that will continue to influence my design work far into the future.

For many of us to feel truly content in life, we must constantly be creating, continually refining that quality of life that is preoccupied with harmony, structure, and beauty—those intangible things that educate and delight us. Yet I know there are times when we plan our houses as much for the pleasure of our friends as for ourselves, because we wish for their enjoyment, and rely on their appreciation and praise—especially their praise. Thankfully that stage of my life has passed! Today, I am far more interested in a home only for myself and those I share my life with. A house is what we design and decorate to suit an image of ourselves, and a home is what we establish by actually living there. To be at home in our house is ultimately the reward of all the effort and thought we put into that most private process of decorating.

There are those who spend lifetimes in houses that have nothing to do with who they really are. They may be perfectly designed, yet if they fail to reflect the personalities of the people who live in them, the very essence of intimacy is missing, and this absence is disturbingly visible. Houses that we call *too decorated* lack the very ingredients that make a home come alive. Our private house should be a reflection of ourselves, our way of being in the world, what makes us distinctly different from one another. Taste is a matter of opinion and its nature is constantly seeking to define itself. So we are continually influenced by the people we meet, by what we read, and by what we see. Our opinions take shape, yet we are never fully formed, always becoming, incorporating experiences, continuously changing and refining our image of ourselves throughout our lives. This never-ending process of evolvement makes designing one's own home an extremely personal experience.

This book describes my experiences as a designer, an antiques dealer, and a creator of wallpapers, furniture, fabrics, and anything I can imagine that will add to the everyday luxury of living. As I have always had an aversion to the concepts of *in style* and *out of style,* and any doctrines that pertain to decoration, I most definitely do not presume to present you with any rules about design. Instead, the chapters that follow reveal, sometimes in the form of daily notes, the impressions that inform my judgment and taste. Again, only you can accurately express your uniquely individual identity. You may choose from those personal sources of inspiration that interest and inspire you, and ultimately those choices will be what combine to create your private house.

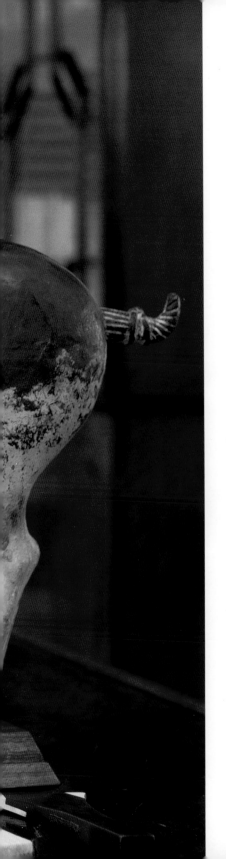

My Father's House

There have been times when I have lain in bed longing for the lost loves of my childhood, my father and our house, and the feeling of protection they gave me. They were the foundations of my world. So many of those memories continue to linger, sometimes in dreams so real that I wake up expecting to be in my father's house, a house that I have never stopped trying to replace. Everywhere I have ever lived since then has been a work in progress, for that particular private house is forever fixed in my heart.

My father bought his house without ever having seen it. He asked an agent to find him the largest property that was available on the ocean. The agent found exactly that, and my father purchased our family house for a price that would not buy a luxury car today.

It was white with a red tile roof and wide, luxurious porches. It sat far from the main road, up a very long and winding tree-lined private

drive. A prominent limestone plaque over the front door read WINDRIFT 1903. The lawns in front of the property extended to Ocean Avenue. A carpet of smooth, flat grass behind the main house stretched out to the Atlantic Ocean. To the side of the property, reflecting the design of the main residence, stood another building, whose ground floor was the garage; the gardeners' and staff quarters were situated above. Greenhouses, orchards, and kitchen gardens surrounded it, all separated from the main residence by a brilliant green lawn and tall formal hedges.

Clipped into huge, round shapes, these hedges were quite hollow inside so that we children could gather within for private club meetings. The potting sheds, greenhouses, and kitchen gardens were close to the garage area, and on the side of the main house were sunken rose gardens, surrounded by long, rambling, rose-covered stone walls. A stone and bronze sundial stood in the middle of the hedged-in flower beds, and inscribed on it was the familiar reminder: TIME AND TIDE WAIT FOR NO MAN. All four corners of the garden had symmetrical and identical carved stone seating arbors, entirely covered by pale-colored climbing roses. As teenagers we would meet in these secluded arbors and secretly puff on cigarettes, confident that we were out of sight. Beyond the rose garden were clay tennis courts that overlooked the ocean. Inside, I would sit by my bedroom window and stare for hours at that endless expanse of water, dreaming fantastic, fanciful dreams, some of which may even have come true.

Windrift had four floors of living space. The top two floors held twenty bedrooms, including guest rooms and playrooms. At the very top of the house, under the roof, was an artist's studio with a long, low, slanted window facing the ocean. One morning, my brother was playing there with a chemistry set and accidentally started a small fire. My sister ran all the way down to the ground floor to find my mother. By the time they rushed back up to the top floor, my brother had put out the fire and run off to hide, which he did quite easily in an immense Chinese cloisonné pot that, even when filled with palms, could conceal a child. When my mother came into the room, all she saw were Larry's shoes lying next to a heap of smoldering ashes on the floor. Thinking that he had been burned right down to his sneakers, she fainted. The next week a tiny elevator was installed.

Windrift was purchased completely furnished. Only a few architectural changes were made, and one of them was to enlarge the pantry by making the dining room smaller. The original kitchen occupied much of the ground floor. It was a vast working kitchen, clad in sparkling white tile, with tall, deep, walk-in steel refrigerators. Unused meat hooks hung from the walls. There were wood-topped preparation areas, and an old dumbwaiter, strictly out of bounds to children, that went up and down between the pantry and the floor above. Our new kitchen was a practical, modern kitchen with an adjoining children's dining room. The original kitchen was used only by the staff, for storage, and as a large-scale preparation area for entertaining.

The lower floor of the house also had a staff dining room with a window seat that looked out to the service courtyard. In addition, on that lower level was a wine cellar with several rooms, a repair shop, a laundry room, an ironing room, and an oil burner that was the size of a baby blimp but never really performed its heating job properly.

One of the difficulties of living on the ocean was the dampness of the northern winter months. The paint on the walls was forever peeling, inside and out, and the rooms either had to be heated all winter long to prevent this or repainted every spring. My father decided it was far more sensible to have the walls continually repainted than to try to keep that temperamental old oil burner working, so it was possible to choose a new bedroom paint color practically every year. I was the only one in a family of five children who had any interest in doing this. I was so much more comfortable when my bedroom was just right—even the seashells on my mantel were constantly being shuffled about. Not satisfied with stopping there, I would go about the whole house, moving and rearranging things.

My mother was well aware of my discriminating nature and encouraged me. She would often ask me to check the appearance of the house before a party. I would look carefully through the rooms that the guests would be entertained in, adding and rearranging as I went along.

On the first floor of the house was an enormous entry hall with rows of French doors that led out to the terrace. Centered in front of the doorways was a big carved walnut hall table. In winter, the chairs and sofas on either side of the room were covered with a heavy, flame-stitched velvet fabric, and in summer they were slipcovered in a solid, bone-colored linen. The coffered wood ceiling had once had a design on it, but I can barely remember the pattern, for it was painted over when I was too young to have paid attention.

To the left of the entry hall was the dining room, made smaller because of the enlargement of the pantry-kitchen, but still very sizable by today's standards. It was thought to have been improved with the addition of a large picture window that opened to a view of the lawn stretching down to the ocean. Though I could not have explained it, I instinctively knew that this window was out of keeping with the architecture of the house, but the magnificent view of the ocean it offered had the power to take my breath away. A long, formal dining table seated at least twenty of us every day, for the houseguests who came to visit with their children and children's governesses often stayed the entire summer.

In the evening, tables for card parties were set for the adults in the living room, which was situated on the right side of the entry hall. The room had not very attractive marble busts sitting on the heavy marquetry and ormolu stands that had come with the house. My memory of the original fabric on the upholstered furniture has faded, but somewhere in its history the room was painted white, and all the upholstered pieces were covered in a pale steel-blue damask. From the living room one could enter the glassed-in sunporch, with its large bar and masses of sofas, tables, and chairs, all made of 1920s vintage bamboo; as teenagers, we had our summer parties there.

When we first moved to Windrift it was our family's main residence, but eventually we used it only as a summer house, for we children went off

OVERLEAF) **A Knole sofa in my living room dates back to the seventeenth century. It still has its original covering of worn velvet and intricate embroidery.**

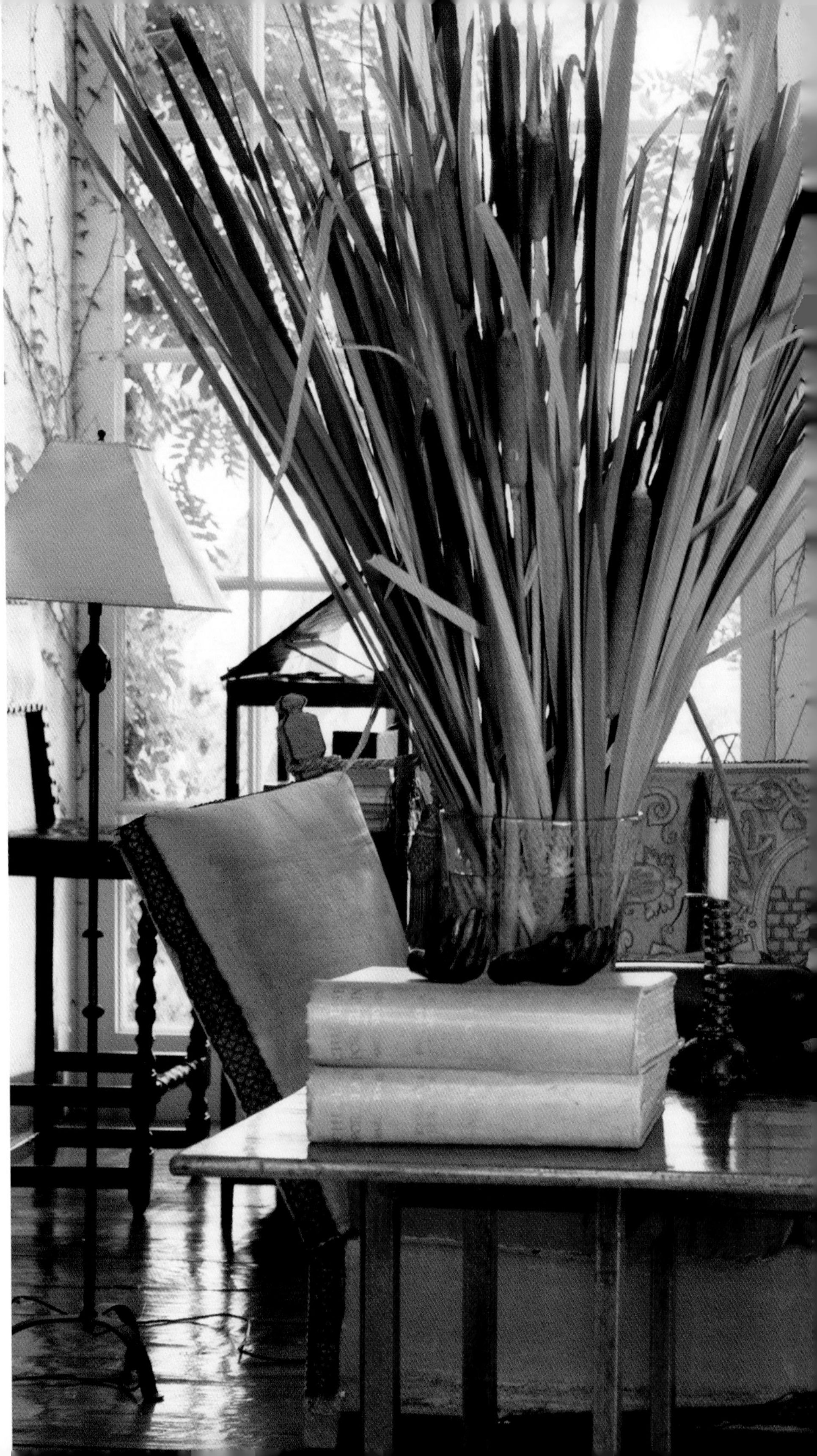

to boarding school and my parents spent the winters in Manhattan and Florida. After the loss of my father, Windrift became an enormous responsibility for my mother to handle alone. Such grand old houses had become white elephants by then, because it was no longer reasonable to retain the large staffs they required.

Slowly the house began losing its perfectly pristine and cared for beauty. Its rooms were repainted every few years instead of every spring. Small areas of paint would peel and would have to be scraped away; then the scraped places would have to wait for months, till it was time for the whole house to receive its new coat. A man seated on a tractor mowed the lawn, instead of the gardeners who always had carefully manicured it in the past. Cracks in the clay tennis courts sprouted tiny weeds, which would have once been rolled away with a large iron roller. The sunken flower and rose gardens were still maintained, but the berry orchard and the kitchen gardens were greatly diminished.

One of the last scenes of Windrift in my memory is of that marvelous outdoor porch facing the ocean. I can still see the two large English baby prams covered with fine, white netting, one containing my baby son Glen and the other holding my niece Jacqueline. My husband is occupied, skillfully hitting old golf balls into the ocean, and from the distance I can hear the laughter and chatter of other family members playing tennis.

The house burned down in an electrical storm before I turned twenty. It happened during the winter, when we were away. The top two floors were completely destroyed; the main floor survived, though many of its furnishings were charred and soaked. Looters stole the carpets from the entry hall and the living room, but because of their great size they were found a week later at a carpet-cleaning facility in the next state. The surviving furniture was dispersed among the family; we still have some cherished pieces, but many personal mementos were lost forever. Perhaps the house could have been rebuilt, but it was far too large, and we were all young and eager to move on to more modern lifestyles. It is difficult to think about that time of my life without a deep, bittersweet sadness.

The years spent at Windrift provided the groundwork for my life and my work. I have carried my memories, my fragments of that house, like a child's soft blanket, into my adult life.

A private house: The house I live in now has also come to mean a great deal to me, perhaps because it is the first house I actually built for myself. Toward the end of the 1980s, I was involved in the design of a particularly large project for a client. When this house was finally completed, I felt in need of a new creative adventure. My shop kept me busy, and for that reason I did not want to embark on another professional design project. I had found a hillside property filled with trees, and so began the most exciting endeavor I have ever experienced—a house built for me. For the first time, I had no one to answer to, not a partner, not a client, and not an architect. And this project slipped in just under the wire, for a few months after completing it, I began a personal relationship with an architect. Had we met earlier, it is certain I would have missed the solitary design experience.

With only myself as designer and client, my imagination and budget were my only constraints. I tore down the structure that had been on the property and began planning my house. An engineer signed the technical plans required, but I did the design and supervision myself. In fourteen months the entire project was completed. Had anyone else been involved, it would have taken years longer.

In designing the house, I studied the California houses built by Wallace Neff, with their dark beams and high ceilings. They seemed to fit perfectly in the lush landscape, and this type of architecture would suit me quite well—old California, with a very strong European influence.

It was important to me not to have a poorly contrived old feeling in a new house, so I found and imported almost everything I needed, primarily antique salvage materials. As an antiques dealer I knew exactly where to look. My first purchase was from England: six long, heavy oak beams that had originally been used in an eleventh-century church in Kent. They pointed the house in the direction it was to take. I found smaller beams in Europe to create other ceilings. (They lay around the property before being installed, looking not unlike an order of Chinese

RIGHT) In spring, the vines in my living room become a curtain to be gently held aside when passing from one part of the room to another. OVERLEAF) The other end of my living room, at another time of the year. The large drawing above the fireplace is by Jean Cocteau, drawn by the artist on a wall in Paris. This is an actual part of the wall, which was removed and framed.

spareribs.) Old wood is highly valued in Europe for repairing and making furniture and is thus hard to find.

Early in the development stages of the house, four pairs of eighteenth-century French oak doors were incorporated into the design for the living room. Then came the discovery of a wonderful arched door and casement, as well as all the other antique doors and old hardware needed for the house. With the exception of the exterior doors and windows, most of the materials were brought over from Europe and refitted in Los Angeles, including part of an eighteenth-century pine room that had been practically abandoned in a warehouse in the French countryside. This meant that my bedroom and bathroom could be paneled and finished in a rich, deep-honey color, which I preferred over bleaching wood to a light pine color, as would have been the conventional solution. The *boiserie* was not quite enough to fill the bedroom or to continue into the other areas, so my dressing room was built using additional antique pine that was designed to join and blend into the bedroom (see page 70). The floors of my studio upstairs are seventeenth-century slate, and the dining room and kitchen have very old stone floors in shades of gray and sand.

I visited the construction site twice a day to inspect, approve, redesign, and muse—it was a thrilling time. The house was soon over budget, but part of the pleasure of building a project should be walking onto the construction site and changing a space or adding a window. Being restricted to a firm blueprint is like taking the chisel out of the sculptor's hands in the middle of a work in progress. We should expect changes when designing or building a house. It may be a once-in-a-lifetime pleasure, and one that should be savored with all its magical possibilities. And hire the finest craftsmen possible. Although it may not seem cost effective early on, ultimately it is a decision that one cannot afford not to make.

The Perfect Puzzle

The architecture of a space should be as perfect as possible, and should look that way. Furniture and accessories must also be considered with great care and attention, but should not seem so. This interplay of evident perfection and seeming spontaneity best begins with a floor plan. Many find intense pleasure in concentrating on a difficult crossword puzzle; my favorite type of puzzle is the planning of a particular space on paper.

Last fall, during the many hours spent on a plane from Marseilles to Manhattan, I worked and reworked the floor plan of a farmhouse I had seen in Provence. Curled up in my seat, I thought about the large barn that belonged to a neighbor but was attached to this house. I know this sounds unusual, but I have since discovered that it is not uncommon in Provence for neighbors to own buildings on one another's property. The entire ground-floor plan had potential. The small stone-floored entry hall was enormously charming just as it was, suggesting the comfort and pleasure promised within. In the center, I could picture a round hall

PRECEDING PAGE) A projection
room such as this one often
serves several needs. There
should be an abundance of
comfortable chairs, which
makes a flexible floor plan
essential. It's a puzzle to be
worked and reworked to
accommodate movie viewers
and to take into account those
times when the room is used
for a less specific purpose.
ABOVE) This guest powder
room off the projection room
was constructed by redesign-
ing several tiny, uninteresting,
wallpapered rooms. The
figured, articulated ash
walls make it as dramatic
as the films shown in the
adjoining room. RIGHT) A
Pierre Chareau bench makes a
fine sculpture.

table with a big glazed bowl filled with lovely fragrant lavender. Maybe a worn white-and-gray-blue linen rug would sit under the table, along-side a chipped, chalky, painted bench, heaped with finely woven baskets for gathering flowers, voluptuous straw bonnets, and a stack of soft cotton quilts for picnics on the grass.

Try to imagine it, to feel its magic. In this house, the living room, kitchen, and dining room could become one open, unobstructed space with a comfortable new layout. In my mind's eye, I could picture a big, cozy kitchen: see the sunlight filter in through the panes of the window; smell the scent of drying herbs and baking bread; taste the pear-and-almond tart prepared for afternoon tea on the heavy wooden table in front of the centuries-old stone fireplace—these dreams and design choices were the adrenaline that sustained me for the long air journey.

The plan to make the kitchen and dining room into one room came from a particularly magical dinner we had attended a few nights before at the house of some friends who had served an early supper in their country kitchen. It was the kind of kitchen that perfectly captured my dream of Provence: a rectangular room with a big, long, wooden country table in the center, lovely old pots on open shelves, an ancient stone fireplace where meals had once been cooked by the women of the farm, and glass jars of fruits and vegetables lining the walls, as they had done for many centuries in the past.

Against the walls of the kitchen were several work tables. Hanging beneath one of them was a shirred curtain of heavy blue-and-white checked linen, parted on both sides to reveal a dog sleeping quietly. It resembled a canopy bed, except that the top of the canopy was a work space. In another corner of the kitchen a plump, silver-streaked cat was curled up in a cozy basket under her own canopy. Under a window there was a rough stone sink large enough to bathe a cow.

Our supper was served with such ease that I was curious to discover how it was accomplished. The usual evidence of kitchen work was nowhere to be seen. While it appeared that a portion of the meal was being prepared in our midst, this was just an illusion; all that sat on the old stove was a pot of *pistou,* country vegetable soup with the subtle flavor of basil and garlic. The rest of the dinner was served from a painted gray-blue sideboard that held a tray of country cheeses, a cake, and a beautifully woven basket filled with garden fruit. There were no utensils or messy dishes to be found anywhere; everything was neat and picture-perfect yet we were dining in the kitchen. Intriguing!

After a bit of examination, I noticed there was actually a tiny pantry just off the kitchen that held a counter, a secondary small stove, and yet another stone sink, sitting on a heavy, wooden work table. There may also have been a refrigerator, but it was not in evidence, for all the appliances in this kitchen that were less than a hundred years old were tucked away behind doors or counter-height shirred curtains.

This idyllic setting gave me food for thought while working on the farmhouse floor plan. Why have a separate dining room and kitchen in the new house? Why not simply add a tiny service pantry that could be used for occasional cooking and washing up when entertaining friends? The spacious kitchen would open during the warm months onto the garden, where an outdoor dining table and chairs would be placed. This would leave the kitchen table free for us to use in buffet style. In the cold weather, we could have our meals in the kitchen, warmed by the fire. The large table could also be used as a desk, or just another place to paint, draw, or read. This farmhouse was to be a family vacation house where entertainment would be both casual and intimate. In the event that there needed to be help with the serving, it could be carried out unobtrusively from the service pantry. With this plan, it would be quite

LEFT) I can just see this bar
filled with beautiful people,
as it must have been in the
heyday of Hollywood. The
shape is the same, but the
paneling and moldings have
been changed.

simple for anyone to perform a multitude of culinary miracles almost invisibly.

The first floor would then have the entry, a small powder room, and the luxuriously large eat-in kitchen with its pantry and laundry service area. The addition of the neighbor's barn, with its original walls and timbers kept intact, would allow me to build a wonderfully high-ceilinged new living room. On the second floor of the farmhouse, the many minuscule bedrooms and one bathroom could be turned into three bedrooms and three baths.

I worked ecstatically on the floor plans for the entire plane trip, and for days after. At night, thinking of the floors, furniture, and fabrics, I slept restlessly, dreaming of design ideas.

Alas, the house was not to be. The farmer on the neighboring property would not part with his barn, and that addition had been essential to purchasing the property. My initial sense of loss yielded to the consolation of what was gained: fresh ideas, a keener sense of how to live, a clearer vision of what to look for, and the confidence that another house would present itself at the right moment and offer its own unique possibilities. Yet there are times when I still see myself sitting at a long wooden table with family and friends, preparing and sharing meals in that ancient farmhouse in Provence.

It is absolutely necessary to organize design ideas when working on a floor plan. If you have ever painted a picture or written a story, you will appreciate the process. You begin with a vision and then work toward it, one small step after another. Applying this to a house, you first imagine what you want your room to be like when it is finally finished. A floor plan guides you in getting there, revealing the choices that need to be

Two twentieth-century masters side by side: an armchair by Pierre Chareau and a glass and bronze table by Diego Giacometti.

made in the architecture, the floor coverings, the furniture layout, the wall colors, the fabrics, and ultimately the mood and beauty of the room.

The tools you need are not complicated: a long tape measure; a fresh, full pad of one-quarter-inch graph paper; several sharpened pencils; a quarter-inch scale ruler; and an enormous eraser. A plan is a puzzle that you work and rework until you are satisfied with the results. I would not place furniture or design a room without a floor plan, even if the solutions seem completely obvious. While you are working out your ideas on paper, you may see a way of using the space that is not immediately apparent, and your paper and pencil may discover new possibilities that surpass your most vivid expectations. It is fascinating to uncover what hidden potential a room has to offer. Whenever I am asked to recommend a floor plan, I always answer that I would need to work it out on paper before giving a responsible opinion.

The first step in the planning process is to take accurate measurements of the entire space, including windows, doors, and ceiling heights—every inch is important! The simplest approach is to consider each square on your grid paper as one foot. When designing more than one room, it works well to eventually convert the entire space to a smaller-scale grid to see how the different rooms and halls intersect and interact with each other, but I prefer starting with one room at a time on the one-quarter-inch grid. Working in this larger format allows you to sketch in and move your furniture about with clarity. The first few drawings are for your eyes alone, so you can make as many errors and erase as many times as you like.

But before putting pencil to paper, no matter how eager you are to draw that first line, carefully consider what is expected from the room. Who will be occupying it? When will it be used, and how? Is it a room the family will be together in, or primarily a place for entertaining? Is it a refuge to come to with a book, where one will be quite alone? Is a desk needed? A game table? A tea table, bookcases, storage? Exactly what will this room be inheriting from past rooms and lives? What will hang on the walls? To make an intelligent and accurate plan, consider every possible use. On paper, you can draw the room to scale, including doors and windows, and you can then use overlays of thin tracing paper to avoid having to do it all over for each fresh idea. Also take note of the dimensions of any existing art, carpets, and furniture. After all these measurements are noted, you can begin to work the puzzle.

Now you are ready for your furniture placement. For twenty-five years, the practice of constantly renewing the arrangement of my shop each time a piece is either moved or sold has contributed to the ease with which I can arrange and balance furniture in a room. Sketch in the larger furniture, the anchor pieces, first. These are the soft, upholstered sofas, armchairs, and ottomans that ground the space. Everybody has a particular way of placing furniture. The English, for example, still often place their upright seating, such as camel-back sofas and Queen Anne settees, around the fireplace, and locate the larger, low, soft sofas and upholstered pieces elsewhere in the room.

If a house or apartment has one large, well-proportioned main room, designing it can be a pleasure. If the spaces are poorly proportioned, more ingenuity is needed to create a beautiful space. What are the heights of the ceilings? Are they commensurate with the size of the room? A very large room with a low ceiling can be remarkably uncomfortable and is usually best designed with several seating sections.

If there is a fireplace in the living room, you must consider whether its size and scale are appropriate for the room. Can it produce enough heat and light to truly enhance the room's comfort? Think about where you would want to sit if you were to enter this room with a friend. Where would you sit with a book? Are there a few comfortable reading chairs with good lighting? If there are several readers in the house, can they all quietly pick a spot in the same room without disrupting one another?

Begin with a seating arrangement around the fireplace mantel or facing a view. Many views can be captivating during the day, but consider what will be seen in the evening—even with lighting outside, a window can become a dark abyss. If there is not a beckoning view or other major interest point in the room, such as a fireplace mantel, try to create one with a large cabinet perhaps, or maybe a bank of bookcases.

The focal piece need not be a piece of furniture or a structure against a wall. You may use a large, round table in the middle of a square living room as the object to work your room arrangement around. You could decide to create a secondary seating arrangement and possibly even a

This table is a puzzle that fits together perfectly. Originally from Kew Gardens, England, it is one of the most rare and fascinating pieces of furniture I have ever discovered.

third. It is best to discourage any sense of isolation in a living room. The seating here should encourage a mood of camaraderie—families sharing life, friends visiting. A successful living room is one that is always inhabited. To be in constant use, it must be able to hold most of the activities of daily life—listening to music, watching television, or working on the computer. Use and great care will give it a special patina that defies even dull decoration.

If you have a rug that you are going to use, put it in your plan. If not, sketch in several different-sized carpets—one large enough to take in a full seating area, another just small enough to just fit under the coffee table. When the time comes to shop for floor coverings, it helps to have several different sizes in mind.

In creating preliminary renderings for clients, I like to keep my drawings a bit vague. If they are too precise, I find that the client unconsciously becomes set on duplicating them, and may feel that any change during the course of the project is a compromise. A plan should open up a world of possibilities, but spontaneity and creativity may be lost if you are trying to duplicate any design exactly. Early renderings are usually points of departure, sources for inspiration. (In the same way, the photos in this book are intended as mood creators rather than prototypes of my work; they are meant to stir up feelings of stillness and harmony and possibly to inspire new and different ways of thinking.)

Work and rework the room layout many times, until you have looked at every possible positioning of your pieces. Finally, you may find three ways to arrange a living room. You will be partial to one of the plans in particular. Professionally I have found that it is preferable to present no more than three choices to clients in order to engage them in the process. Considering more than three choices can cause confusion or indecision and is seldom productive.

A fireplace in the living room is always an architecturally and aesthetically pleasing contribution to any space. The presence of a mantelpiece, especially if it is a marvelous one, can be a thing of beauty all year long. When I am at home alone with a book and a tray of tea with a fire blazing away, I may look up at the flames for a moment and be totally transported, dreamily forgetting about everything, including my reading. At this very moment, as I sit writing in front of a huge log fire in the icy cold of an East Hampton Christmas, I am thankful for its waves of heat. I cannot think of any one stroke of magic (except laughter) that can change the ambience of a room as quickly and as potently as a fire blazing and crackling away in the hearth.

A personal rule of thumb, when choosing to place a sofa in front of a fireplace, is to try to locate it approximately eight to ten feet away from

OVERLEAF) **The walls of a small study are covered in glazed leather panels. I designed the desk for this special room.**

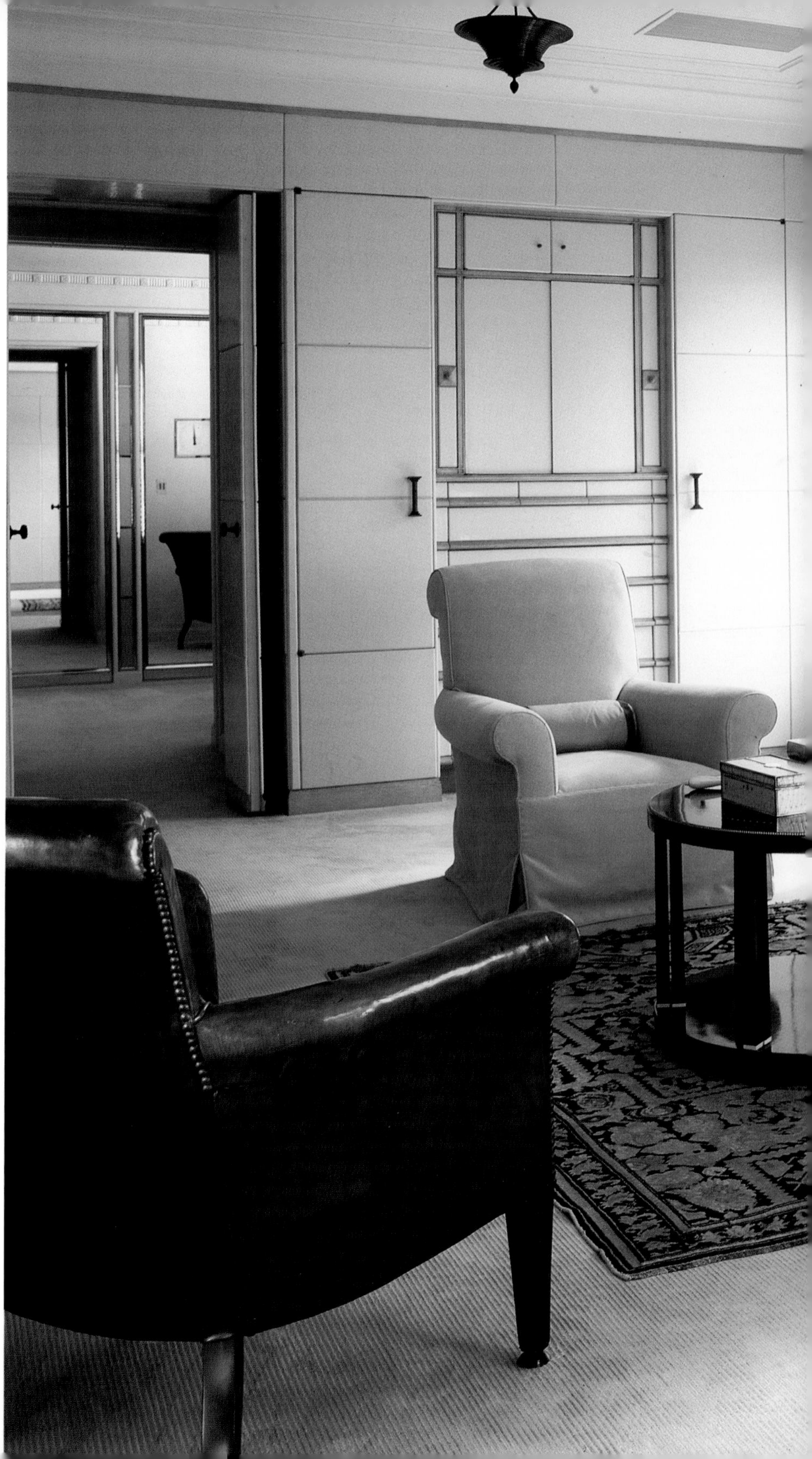

the fire. This distance works perfectly for me: it allows enough space to add cozy, clubby chairs, a coffee table, extra seating, and a pathway for circulation, yet it is just close enough to the hearth for comfort.

Once you have arranged the large, soft, upholstered furniture, such as sofas and club chairs, the next step is to incorporate the smaller-scaled framed chairs and the various tables. These are the objects that help give the room character, distinction, and vitality. Continually move them about in your sketches, striving for optimal flexibility. If this process is neglected, the finished room could easily have a stiffness about it. Whenever you purchase a piece of furniture, always think of several places it could be situated, and anticipate the possibility of changing several other pieces around to accommodate your new object. Remember that there are always many possibilities, each offering a different benefit. The floor plan is the map and the guide that makes this kind of fluidity possible.

After sketching in all the furniture on the plan, begin to envision living in the furnished areas. In a living room, are there enough tables? To be forever holding a cold drink or a hot one without a proper place to set it down is not only extremely inconvenient but will more than likely result in nasty wine or tea stains. It is also disconcerting to be sitting on a deep, comfortable chair or sofa and have to lean down to a low coffee table to spear an olive off a tray miles away, or to lift yourself out of the chair every few minutes to flick an ash. Oriental tables, which are the only authentic antique low tables I know of, were made to be used by persons seated on the floor. While my opinion on this is sometimes considered unorthodox, I prefer to use taller coffee tables. In my house almost all the tables that are in front of sofas are between twenty-four and twenty-eight inches high. Side tables are usually up to thirty inches high. It is easier to reach up than down. Often the coffee and tea tables I design for others are between nineteen and twenty-two inches high, but their height can be changed to suit designers and their clients, and they often are.

Sofa and upholstered seat heights are something else to take into consideration. Not every seat height needs to be uniform, but some conscious thought should be given to the seat, arm, and back heights of upholstered furniture. Some uniformity will help to give a room balance, harmony, and, of course, comfort. I like my soft seating to be a bit higher than normal and all at a somewhat similar height, unless the ceiling in the room is very low. The framed chairs and side tables can, and usually will, be higher still. If all the seat and back heights are the same, the overall look can be flat. Consider all these details on your plan.

As you scan the plan, look to see whether there are too many chair or table legs lurking about. Lots of exposed legs can make a room feel agitated, as if the chairs or tables are untamed gazelles that might just leap up and dance away. What anchors the room is the furniture that is completely upholstered in fabric. The leggy pieces benefit from the stability of the larger, upholstered pieces, and because of their solidity, shapely legs can then dance about with freedom.

The plan is also the perfect place to study the wood pieces in relation to the whole. Are the finishes of the furniture too similar? When designing a deco-style room you could consider having the sofa and chairs and some of the tables all in the same design and wood finish. This is called a suite of furniture and is perfectly appropriate for this period room. Years ago in France, you would often find that the settees and fauteuils (open armchairs) were *en suite* (matching). You can still find these suites in very formal French homes, usually covered in tapestry or heavy silk. Today we try not to have the woods of our furniture pieces all be the same. Their contrasts add an interesting complexity and work to the ultimate compatibility of the whole. Rethink your placement, and create diversity by varying wooden finishes with painted finishes and using lacquer, metal, or stone pieces. Examine the distribution of the furniture on the plan to ensure that the dark-toned or light-toned objects are not all massed at one end of the room. A sense of heaviness at one end and flimsiness at the other gives the room the feeling of a tipping ship. Are the tall or very large pieces somewhat in balance? For example, if there is to be a piano at one end of the room, you may try a cabinet, a sofa, a large sculpture, or a tall screen at the other end. Is the room top-heavy or bottom-heavy? Unless consciously planned, too much uniformity can be monotonous and produce a flat overview, especially if everything is the same height or size. It is not necessary for everything to be in balance, but do be aware of these questions. Again, the plan tells all.

Detailed planning may sound contrived, and it is. But a room must *be* comfortable in order to look comfortable. In this, the eye cannot be fooled. Comfort is not to be taken for granted and it should be carefully

ABOVE) I found a pair of period archways and reworked them to create a dressing room and bath that became a continuation of the master bedroom.
RIGHT) A contemporary painting hangs over the fireplace mantel in this master bathroom directly across from the bathtub, which has a view of the garden.

thought out. However, flexibility is essential, for if a plan is not open to change, the room will feel, look, and be rigid and self-conscious. Far from being fixed, the floor plan is a constantly updated picture of considerations to keep in mind. Perfection can be boring, but ignorance is rarely bliss.

The plan will also help balance and layer the fabrics and colors chosen for the space. Eventually, you will look at all the fabrics and colors in relation to the entire design. Not unlike painting a picture, first you may sketch your room in black and white and then fill in the colors, layering and building on a premeditated concept.

After arranging furniture on the floor plan, consider where to incorporate the lighting. Quite soon you will need a comprehensive lighting plan that shows where the electrical equipment and outlets will be placed for ambient, practical, and atmospheric lighting. Pieces that sit away from the perimeter of a room may require a light source to be plugged in nearby. In new construction, I would put these plugs underneath the furniture. This should be decided upon in advance and the wiring added before the floors are laid. On your graph paper, place table lamps and floor lamps next to the chairs that may be suitable for reading and then consider whether the lighting is dispersed at different levels yet somewhat evenly throughout the room.

Living rooms should have long ago ceased to be rooms kept for special occasions, but many of the most elaborate ones do not look lived in, simply because they are not. If all your furniture is quite serious, spread it throughout the house or, better yet, let some of it decorate an auction house or an antique shop. Too many self-important pieces in one place can keep a room from looking young and fresh, not unlike a woman wearing too much important jewelry. In every aspect of decorating,

PRECEDING PAGE) I designed
this very masculine bed with a
Palladian influence for a master
bedroom. RIGHT) A master bath
vanity with charming old ivory
grooming accessories.

there may be the temptation to use too much of a good thing: resist. Be ruthlessly discerning in your placement of treasures. Wonderful pieces are made even more strikingly special when they stand center stage and do not have to compete for attention.

Freedom from formality does not mean unsophisticated. But what does it mean when a room or a piece of furniture is described as *sophisticated*? To me, sophistication is a perfect marriage between intelligence and simplicity, combined with supreme confidence. A sophisticated room is simple in form and line. Its quality and elegance are subtle and self-assured. When a piece of furniture, a painting, or an accessory is put in a room with the intention of creating a special or eccentric effect, what you end up with is an affectation, which jolts instead of pleases. Eccentricity in design is unique and special only when it comes from within you, sometimes unintentionally, quite often irrationally, and always for the right reasons.

Color and Light

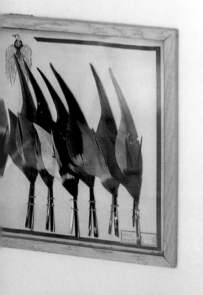

Provence: I am here for a few weeks primarily to concentrate on my writing. It is early October and the weather is truly glorious. It is clear why so many artists have come to this region of France to paint: the light is translucent.

Each morning, I walk a short distance from the house where I am staying into the village of Eygaliers. I pick up the newspaper at the Maison de Presse and sit at the same café, where I order my café crème. It is a bit cool and I am the only one seated outside, with the exception of a very old French man. He talks to his dog and I talk to myself. This is heaven—the only thing I have to do in the next few hours is buy a baguette and some cheese before the small markets close for lunch. At this very moment I am sitting looking at a blank page.

At the top of the page I write the word *Color*. I look up at the sky, then back at my page, and cross the word out and replace it with *Light*. I look down the street. Two dogs are playing. A woman bent over her

bike pedals by, a colorful purple-and-pink woolen scarf tied under her chin, her basket of groceries dangling on the curve of the bike's handlebars. My eyes move to one of the village houses. It is ancient, brittle, and worn, yet beautiful. Its tall shutters are an uncommon shade somewhere between blue and green, mellowed by years of sunlight and the winds of the mistral. I must hold this color in my memory. I cross out the word *Light* on top of my still blank page and reinstate *Color*. My eyes take in the soft hues of the old buildings and the Roman-built stone road. Eygaliers is a small, humble village with houses of varied articulated shapes and heights pressed tightly against each other. I keep returning to the shutters. How can I describe them? If you were to mix the watercolors Prussian green and Prussian blue, it might be just the right shade. The color thrills me. Would I be as captivated if all the shutters of the village were painted this color? I think not. Part of what is so captivating is the singularity.

Color can be a powerful factor in any interior. In fact, it may be the most important design decision we may make. It is essential, then, to spend time with a color, become preoccupied with it before making a commitment to live with it. Look at it at different times of the day to see if your feelings about its beauty are the same after a few days or weeks. Revisit it at dusk, in the evening, and in the sunlight.

There is no color under the sun that is not perfection when it is used with a discriminating eye. Yet we all have colors we love working and living with and those that we are not at all at peace with. In any artistic endeavor, color has so much power that even as tiny a color spec as a ladybug can create a new picture. We are the painters of our own worlds, and nature is the most brilliant artist of all. If you are at all intimidated about using color, you may find it instructive to study tropical fish—a bold and wondrous palette, to be sure. The colors are so vivid they transcend the capacities of human inspiration.

To appreciate color, look at trees on the street, how they are silhouetted against the sky; some branches are bare and some are heavy with leaves, pattern on pattern, color on color. If you have windows in your house framing the sky, a tree, or even a building, you have a complete collage of color in your room. On any one day, the sky may be blue, white, silver, or many shades in between; there is no work of art that can do what a window can do.

Many of the rooms I have designed have a simple background wash of color, but this does not mean I do not appreciate color. Just the opposite: I need color in my life for visual nourishment, and so I use it with great discretion and respect. I often prefer to use various shades of one unifying color throughout the main rooms of an apartment or house. Unexpected accents of color can be added with objects: a beautiful old fragment of fabric on a chair, an unusual Oriental vase, a piece of painted furniture, a patterned area rug, a painting, a wonderful collection of books, a stunning lacquer box, a table or a cabinet that adds some new color complexity. In this way, I am continually engaged in experiencing a variety of different shades without ever feeling wedded to a single one. You will find you are passionate about different colors at different times, and you may enjoy experimenting with a variety of them. Consider, therefore, giving yourself a neutral canvas to work with and use color as if it were jewelry: provocatively.

I remember designing an apartment with a long hallway that jutted off clumsily in several directions. To transform the hall from a difficult walkway to a visually interesting gallery of turns was a challenge that I resolved by laminating the walls with a deep, rich, cinnabar-colored cotton chamois cloth. The rest of the apartment was in soft tones of

toast, with accents of completely different shades of red: a Chinese red-lacquered coffee table; a Bessarabian rug with some brown and slightly brick-red tones; Italian dining room chairs painted a very old, worn Venetian red; and in the bedroom, a delicate printed fabric that had small bits of vermilion and peach in it. All these very different variations on red were united by the richly colored hallway, so the adjoining rooms were in continuous accord with one another. The small apartment looked larger than it actually was because it was not broken up by different color palettes. From within any of the neutral-colored rooms, small glimpses of the hallway were experienced as splashes of flickering flame, sometimes entering into the room and sometimes not, depending on where you were standing and at what angle light hit the hallway. A collection of drawings framed in black and gold that hung on its walls

Influenced by my trip to Ireland, I was determined to use an abundance of green in this pool house. Dick Tracy is such a powerful presence in the space that strong color was needed to make a balancing contribution to the room.

RIGHT) An antique Chinese table holds a few marvelous treasures—an enormous Japanese ivory crayfish, garden roses, and bronze and alabaster antiquities. OVERLEAF) Melrose House twisted twig chairs are placed around an old stone table, which faces a wisteria-covered stone fireplace.

were haloed in color, appearing far more interesting cloaked in cinnabar than they actually were. Nothing detracted from the sense of harmony. The difficult, odd hall had become a gay, eccentric ribbon that united the rooms.

Trying to reinstate or *match* a strong wall color in your furniture or fabrics almost always makes a room look contrived. Instead, it can be far more provocative to introduce many different shades of the same tone. This technique of varying shades can be used to advantage in any area of color coordination. On a table in front of me sits a bowl of roses from the garden. I do not often mix flower colors in one arrangement, but I have put the varieties Apricot Brandy and Just Joey together in the bowl. Their petals contain many gradations of color: orange, amber, maize, apricot, flame, and even a spot of rusty red. Together, the subtle combination of shades make the tiny bouquet strikingly beautiful.

Thinking back to red, let us say you decide to paint your walls a red

that has a brick tone, sometimes described as oxblood, Chinese red, Indian red, or brown madder Alizarin, a watercolor from my paintbox that is a red with no blue undertones. Perhaps your plan will be to use pink with it, a pink that also contains no blue—a salmon pink, for example. Other shades of red could be used to cover some of the furnishings, perhaps a wonderful chintz whose different colors include a brown to relate to the red terra-cotta tones in the walls. Every color has complex tones that may be able to work together. Think of the variety of greens in a garden—there is not one shade, but many: the grass, the different trees, the flower stems, the vines. Everywhere you look you find varying shades of the same color; there is no exact match, just the perfect pigments of nature.

We can recall shades that have special associations for us. I associate yellow with the first house I lived in as an adult. Before I lived in it, I admired the house from the outside and would drive by quite often. It

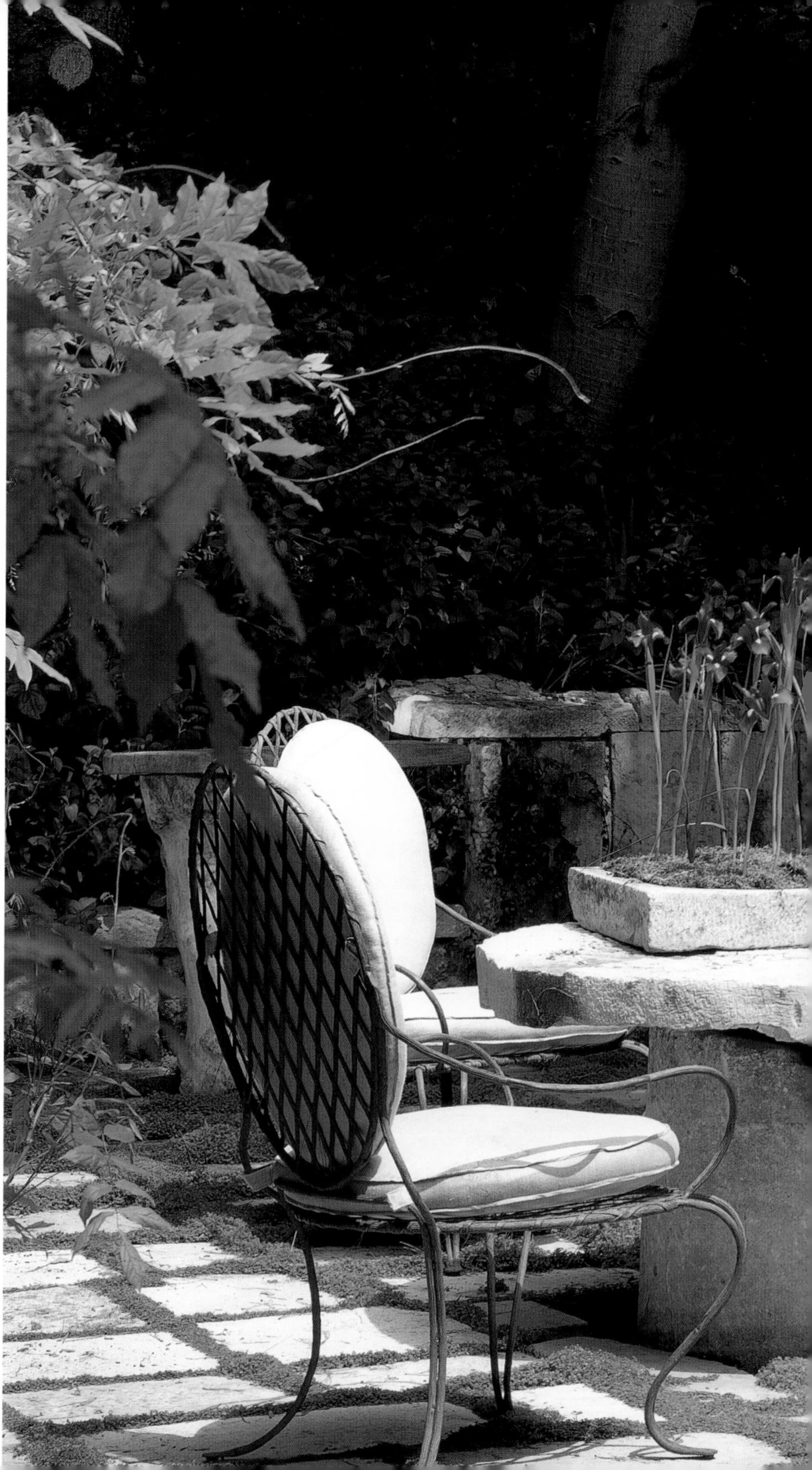

LEFT) In a bath, dressing, and sitting room adjoining the master bedroom, a chaise faces the fireplace.

BELOW) There are so many ravishing textures and colors in this bedroom and dressing room: the *boiserie* walls, the lacquer of the William and Mary secretary, the original tapestry covering the Régence fauteuil, the gilding on the Régence mirror, the Rodin watercolors, the hammered satin bed covering, and the print on the chintz bed hangings.

was an exquisite Tudor-style house with a vine-covered turret. One day I saw the owner outside gathering his mail and I stopped to speak to him. I asked if he knew of any houses on the street that were for sale; he was so gruff that I did not dare be too specific. Months later, on one of my drives past the house, I saw him again, and this time when we spoke I found that he had mellowed slightly. His wife had died, and he was thinking of selling the house. But surely I was far too young to have a house as special as this one, he observed. It was too late: I had already made a decision, and eventually the house was ours. Our first night there, we invited a neighbor for a drink and were told that the former owner's wife had hung herself in the turret! My winding stairwell never quite felt the same again.

Because the interior rooms of this house had a strong architectural presence, color was used in a very controlled and minimal way. The brightest and best space was a charming room off the living room. It had a high wooden truss ceiling and milk-paint-white walls of lightly textured plaster. The wood beams and floorboards were dark, old, and beautiful, and three of the walls had tall, leaded-glass windows, as did almost all the windows in the dimly lit house. I upholstered the furniture in a heavy, cola-colored linen and added lots of white and many bright yellow pillows, a white lacquered bamboo chair covered in brown and white cowhide, and a slick brown-and-white zebra rug on the floor. The yellow I used gave a tremendous lift to the deep tones. Remembering that room now, I think I would most likely arrange it the same way today.

Not so for the dining room, however. There, I painted all the woodwork a flat black, and used a stunning flat-black wallpaper covered with orange-and-rust-colored palm fronds. White Chippendale-style chairs (the chairs from my very first apartment) made for a very striking effect, but the result was a room we rarely used. While it was magical and dramatic at night—all candlelit and glowing—by day it was gloomy and far too sophisticated for a young family with tiny tots and sticky fingers.

When I think of yellow, I always envision a field of tiny buttercups. The yellow I use is close to maize and without green undertones. Yellow is a touch of sunlight wherever it is placed, and indoors it glows, even at night. In my house today, my bedroom and dressing room have wood paneling on the walls, and the furniture is slipcovered in pale yellow linen. A delicate floral fabric hangs on the four posts of the canopy bed and at the windows. Many of the wood pieces in the room are black lacquered chinoiserie, which looks amazing with the yellow fabrics and the wood walls.

Just as color and light are close companions, so too are color and texture. We should devote a great deal of attention to background textures. For me, the very best walls are usually simple and clean, most often with only a single color or texture throughout. Lacquered colors on walls can work wonderfully in deeper colors. Today, dark walls are not used as often as in the past. Times change, and tastes move through cycles, styles all but disappearing and then reappearing quite unexpectedly. When I did work with dark walls, I preferred them slightly textured. I would paper walls in line-textured paper or in a very flat-textured hessian cloth, and then paint over them a deep matte color; over this, I'd apply a coat of varnish. The reason for this complicated process is that, for me, a plain dark lacquered wall can look a bit too slick and too dramatic in daylight. I find that in time, the shine and the drama become intrusive.

Just before the holidays, the painting contractor I have worked with for years stopped by the shop. For quite some time he had been telling me about the wallpaper he had removed from a client's house. I was interested in this, as my painter friend had taken a portion of the paper to one of the auction galleries and had been assured that it was quite valuable. When he brought in a panel to show me, it was a great surprise, for it was from a room I had designed in our old Rockingham Road house in Brentwood. This was where my children grew up, a lovely white brick traditional family house that had been built by the architect Paul Williams for Za Su Pitts, a Hollywood actress of the 1930s and '40s.

I have always had a passion for eighteenth-century wallpapers, which are difficult to find. So, based on my research on rare Chinese wallpapers, I had commissioned an artist to handpaint wallpaper panels, adding a few more birds, putting the flowering trees in Chinese blue-and-white pots, and editing out some of the flowers that are found in such profusion in traditional papers. As with fine antique furniture, I have such a reverence for the authenticity and age of the original that I do not focus on changing any specific detail when designing new versions. Instead, I find myself trying to improve upon the scale, or simplifying the design. Just because a piece is old does not necessarily mean that it is well designed. For every gem of antique furniture, there are hundreds of antiques that are not what we would wish them to be. This fact is often ignored, perhaps because the patina of age adds something special, or because the piece is just quirky enough to become a treasure nonetheless. In any case, we tend to ignore the fact that all that is old is not always beautiful. I would rather have a splendid, well-designed, newly made piece of furniture than a period antique that is poorly proportioned and not all that interesting.

I remember waiting ages for the panels to be painted and hung. At last the room was finished, and it was breathtaking. The first evening it was completed we all sat for hours admiring the walls, but I could not wait

Chinese wallpaper is always my favorite. The lacquer cabinet, dining table, and chairs are from Melrose House. The mirrors and large cabinet are English.

to be alone in the room. Later that night, when the family was asleep, I went back down to the dining room, took 00 sandpaper, fine steel wool, a stepladder, and all of my nerve and proceeded to soften the newness of the paper by removing some of the design. I worked slowly and carefully for hours, and succeeded in completing only a small section. I was pleased with the results. In the morning, my husband, Barry, came downstairs and was horrified. I explained that the work had just begun, but that it needed to be done—the newness of the walls was intruding into the room. They were not the soft and subtle background I wished for.

The artist who produced the panels was recommended by a designer friend of mine, the late Michael Taylor, whom I deeply admired. I probably first began my love affair with Chinese paper in one of his rooms. He liked his papers to look fresh and undistressed, and the artist kept reminding me of this fact. The white backgrounds Michael used on many of his papers were stunning. That was the part of the Michael Taylor magic: his white backgrounds created light and glorious spaces. I was working in an entirely different context. For my room, the paper needed to be soft and muted. We all work differently to attain the same end—beauty, which, as we know, has a different definition for each individual.

When I saw that paper so many years later in my office, I was pleased to know that even the auction house was convinced it was indeed old and rare. It evoked so many memories of that special house and the treasured time in my life when my children were small and I was developing my craft, learning, expanding, experiencing, and growing along with them. Oh, that paper was certainly valuable!

When you study rooms done by the designers of generations past, you will find that many truly memorable ones had remarkably colorful backgrounds. Color-filled rooms can create tremendous impact, and yet there are also times when subtlety can be seductive. It can be creative and fulfilling to work in both contexts. At times I feel energized working with a strong color palette. Then there are other times I want a room to be lighter, fresher, younger, and less dramatic in mood. I suppose I have learned something from my friend Michael Taylor, after all.

English interiors are perfect examples of how comfortable and relaxed our rooms might be, and this is why we are drawn to them. But skillful technique is essential. John Fowler, the master of decorating the English country house, could drag, strié, mottle, or marbleize walls so perfectly that they would be almost agonizingly lovely to look at. In contrast, pseudo-swirled stucco walls that are meant to look old and mellow simply fail miserably.

Not long ago, I accompanied a friend who was looking for a home in London. The real estate market was flooded with flats being bought, refurbished, and then resold. In every newly designed space we entered, we encountered not just one glazed, stippled, mottled, or striéd wall but several different processes executed in several different colors. Every surface would be cloaked in messy color, with not a naked wall in sight. The flavors of the moment seemed to be peach and a watered-down daiquiri. I concluded that I would be much happier never seeing a recently distressed wall again.

While clean, clear walls are refreshing, there are times when you may want to create an aged effect on a plaster wall. My technique for doing so is to mix some garden soil in with my plaster top coat. I put in as much as I need to reach the desired depth of color, though I rarely exceed a measuring cup full. Then I trowel it fairly smoothly. This creates a look that seems far more authentically aged than if you overworked the plaster with swirls and whorls. Soil just seems to have the pigment needed to create a natural-looking aged wall color. It works miraculously

It was a pleasure to work with the architect Charles Gwathmey on this Manhattan apartment. The glare from the large windows is softened by thin slat shades that do not disturb the view in the slightest.

The nightstands on either side of an English four-poster bed in a client's guest bedroom are shown here. The walls have been lacquered in the same time-consuming and handcrafted way that one would lacquer a fine piece of furniture.

with any light and usually needs no other pigments mixed in with it.

To create an uncontrived-looking aged effect on walls, you may also choose to leave out the corner metal stripping that makes edges and corners neat, sharp, and clean. This leaves the walls just slightly irregular, as if carved with a butter knife. I have done this in my own house and love the way it looks. But be aware that any protruding edges constantly have to be patched: no more than a sharp tap may cause an area to crumble. Granted, this may be a bit eccentric, but if you are trying to effect authentically aged wall, patches and unwanted leaks can indeed help to mellow a house naturally. In all cases, a very light hand must be used in purposefully antiquing anything, and that extends to aging fabrics, furniture, wallpaper, and walls. It is similar to applying face foundation—sometimes to get the most natural results, you end up removing half of what you put on.

Simple flat paint can feel clean and fresh, although hallways and entries that endure a lot of use will quickly reveal that flat paint does not bear heavy traffic well. A less delicate paint finish will not only last better but can introduce an interesting texture.

One way of applying flat paint to this end is to use a two-step process, similar to what one would do if a wall was to be stippled. To achieve this, choose two shades of the same color, one darker, one lighter. The first step would be to apply the lighter of the two shades just as you normally would. Then take a clear glaze and infuse it with some of the second, deeper color. The proportions will depend the amount of gloss you want, but the resulting paint will be thin and translucent rather than milky and thick. Paint the wall with this glaze mixture and, while it's still wet, pat the surface with a linen cloth, using very tight, controlled movements so that the mottling is light and fine and the markings are close together. This process is not dissimilar to the process of a stipple finish, yet the end result of this method is even, controlled, and clean looking. The effect hoped for is not that of age but of translucency. If the amount of glaze used is not overwhelming, the wall will not have a noticeable sheen, just a harder surface, rendering the finish less porous and ultimately giving it more staying power. Adding many layers of pigment and using broad strokes in applying the paint only give walls a heavy, uneven, fresco look. Again, too much makeup is not a substitute for a clear complexion.

In what are described as *no-color rooms,* the eye is drawn to the furnishings and objects rather than the room as a whole. Since I am an antiques collector and dealer, furniture is my foremost interest. If a room's predominant color is white, off-white, or any light, neutral tone, then the art, furniture, and accessories will be highlighted. However, it

I find intense beauty in the stillness of the objects in this corner of my kitchen.

can be a challenge to create beautiful colorless rooms without exceptional furnishings. Exceptional does not necessarily mean expensive; it can mean no more than a few simple, well-designed pieces, antique or modern. But have you seen very many neutral-colored rooms with lots of casual clutter and inconsequential furnishings that work well?

Color has a way of enveloping furniture and objects. It is always fascinating to observe what occurs to a space that has strange angles when it is painted, papered, or covered with fabric. There will be an illusion of completeness, even with few furnishings. A wonderful color also enhances a room filled with marvelous furniture, art, and objects. Welcome the opportunity to work in both contexts—rooms filled with color, and rooms that are monochromatic.

Will using color on the walls and on the furniture hide unattractive furniture? *No!* If there are pieces that you do not feel good about having in your house, please do not think they will be camouflaged or glorified by a wash of lavish color. They simply should not litter your life. Color can hide a multitude of sins, but it can not flatter or give stature to pieces that are not meaningful to you.

Using vibrant color in a setting for books can be intensely inviting. Books always look wonderful surrounded by the richness of wood or color. China red, flaming amber, dark woodsy green, and shades of deep cognac are just a few of my favorite background colors for a library. But remember to study these deep colors at all times of the day and night, under both natural and artificial light, since many richly pigmented rooms are more stunning in the evening than when flooded with sunlight. Direct light on a deeply tinted wall will show every flaw and particle of dust. Reflected and diffused light is a bit kinder. Colors will also vary according to the reflectivity of their surface. That is why the same exact shade of a color will always read differently on different textures and surfaces.

Some years ago, for a house situated by the sea, I covered the larger furnishings in the living room in white and used early Bessarabian carpets of a soft wheat color with strands of brilliant green interwoven in the pattern. I wanted the accent pillows that sat nestled on the sofas to evoke the look of crisp lettuce leaves, so I used a thin, crinkly, clear green taffeta that crunched when you handled it. It has been years since the house was designed, and I returned recently to refurbish it, since rooms do not always hold up well near the water. But what I discovered was that I want the rugs to remain in place; the white linen upholstery will be replaced by pale wheat-colored fabric. I still love the lettuce-leaf pillows—they are delicious! Sometimes an unexpected fabric adds the perfect dimension to a room. Though this touch of taffeta might seem formal, it surely does not look that way, as it adds a refreshing crispness and unexpected texture.

Install one room at a time according to the plan, and then invariably you will change it again and again, sometimes editing and at other times kidnapping things that were designated for other rooms to create your picture. You may have to work a bit harder or just completely relax and return after installing another part of the house. This can be alarming at first, until you learn to trust yourself. If you are not ready to finish that area, continue on to another room. Complete it and then return to the uncompleted room. It is a known fact that confidence comes with experience.

For my very own first living room, I painstakingly chose every piece of furniture, carpet, and fabric. However, once the furniture arrived, I was still unsatisfied. It was *too* perfect, brand spanking new and stiff. The minute the delivery men were out the door, immediately and without

A collection of first edition
architecture books on
my library ladder.

any premeditation I began to look for some tools to temper and mellow
the wood. All I could find were tweezers, a hammer, and a wand of mas-
cara. These resulted in my first, and worst, furniture-finishing experiences; when it was over, the pieces looked only marginally better.

Having antiqued the new furniture for the living area, I then proceeded to paint the Chippendale-style dining chairs white. I eventually
found an old dark oak desk in a shop in Greenwich Village. Over the
sofa hung a few pen-and-ink drawings on walls that had been painted a
deep mushroom shade. The entire room now had everything in place,
but something was disturbing me—not wrong exactly, just perhaps too
right. It felt as if we were living inside a shiitake mushroom. I roamed
from room to room, looking for some solution, trying several alternatives, all of which failed to give any immediate satisfaction. Then I settled on a leopard clutch purse purchased in a funky clothing shop. I
stuffed it with tissue, placed it on the sofa, and literally shuddered with

delight. Designers had been using leopard patterns for decades before the creation of my pillow; mine was not an original thought, though I had absolutely no awareness of that. That purse-cum-pillow made the room spring to life. And the feeling of fulfillment it gave me was truly an epiphany.

The most interesting living rooms to see and study are those that have been created by designers, collectors, or artists for themselves; their acquisitive nature, creativity, and personality are revealed. One would imagine that many designers are more controlled when they work with clients than when they are on their own. But when a client and designer work well together, they tend to draw the best from each other, each energizing the process in their own way. A room with its owner's personality indelibly stamped on it will always be fascinating because it is the story of who that person is.

Never leave any room alone until you ignite it. When you complete a house make sure that you have created something quite magical. You will find that the magic rarely comes from where you expect. It is the unexpected, whimsical touches that often give a room its charm.

In my living room I have two Knole sofas. Considered to be the first sofa ever designed, the Knole dates back to seventeenth-century England. My antique sofas still have their original velvet coverings, in colors so muted that they appear to be neutral. Nevertheless, if you look closely at the two sofas, you will see that each is very different in color; one is a delicate blush shade, the peach-rose flush of a baby's cheek, and the other is a shade that would be described as a soft khaki. The two Regency chairs that sit in the middle of the room have slipcovers made of a wonderful old, worn chintz that causes me to melt with pleasure just to look at it. This old beauty of a chintz incorporates different shades of brown, along with some splashes of peach and a very unusual clear shade of pink on a deeply aged and weathered cream ground. Old chintzes can be like rich and luxurious paintings, and I buy special ones whenever I discover them. You may find that you like having chintz in your room in the summer months and then removing it in the fall. Why shouldn't rooms have a seasonal change of wardrobe? This, and the continuous change in flower selection, may be one of the only concessions you make to changing your living room, the room you live in.

When my schedule permits, I teach a master class in design to twelve senior students at UCLA. On every student's project, I expect to see all the fabrics and wall colors to be used applied to a detailed floor plan. The class takes particular interest in studying what will be seen from each doorway. Uncomplimentary or conflicting color changes from room to room can be disturbing to the eye, as can abrupt changes between floor designs and carpets. Clean, flowing areas are disrupted when you look down a hall and see several different floors and carpet patterns unhappily bumping into one another; any connecting areas that are open to other rooms are thus often best left neutral. This consideration establishes continuity and creates harmony.

Recently, however, I had to reconsider this self-inflicted dictate when I visited a very old and beautifully eccentric château in France. Every room had a different stone floor, old and worn and unique, yet the whole was breathtaking. The only disruptive element came in the restoration of one of the rooms with a new tile, antiqued to look old. The abrupt contrast between the antique and the antiqued was truly disconcerting.

As with the vermilion-covered hall I mentioned earlier, you may find that a bold hallway can be interesting when all the rooms that open on to it have a predominantly neutral palette. Then the hallway draws that

PRECEDING PAGE) **With its ancient slate floors and large windows that bring in an abundance of light at all times of the day, my studio is an ideal hideaway that continues to summon creativity.**

space together and functions as an accent. Studying your plan will surely help you make these decisions. I like to have students work with a color board, choosing all the project's wall colors, papers, moldings, ceiling colors, and fabric swatches, and then tacking samples onto the rooms and hallways of a larger scale floor plan. This creates an overview, and allows one to move and change critical elements before they have become long-term commitments.

I have never been one to use different colors on different walls of a room. I have, however, painted different walls in the same space varied shades of the same color. The effect to everybody but myself is indistinguishable. Think of a window that has such an abundance of green reflections flooding in from the garden that the color of one interior wall changes entirely. Reflections can actually make a wall or a corner look as if it is painted a completely foreign hue. In such a case, it may be necessary to change the shade just a bit to bring it in line with the other walls. The objective is not to prevent the colors of the room from changing with the time and light of the day. On the contrary, a play of light on the walls can be natural and magical. The concern enters only if there is an unhappy disruption in the harmony of the whole.

The upstairs portion of my studio has a winding staircase that leads to a sleeping loft (see following page). This loft sometimes acts as an extra guest room, so the windows do at times need to be covered. Hanging from a worn iron rod are very fine linen curtains, the quality of which is difficult to find today. They are extremely old, and in another life they were hemstitched bed linens; I converted them to window hangings by attaching iron rings at the top and letting the hemstitched edge border the side and the bottom. While they do not block out the light totally, they give some protection from the morning sun. The linen was originally a buttermilk color, but when the curtains were actually hanging in the leaded-glass windows, they picked up the reflection of the trees surrounding the house. At once, they appeared to be tinged with green, and next to the wall they had the look of raw, slightly green potatoes. I took them down and tried to modify their color by dipping them in several different tea mixtures. In the end they became a deep shade of cream, a bit closer to the color of the natural plaster wall in the room, which was not what I'd originally intended. Hanging, they still have a hint of green; and in any other instance, I might continue my quest for perfection. But not this time—finally their very imperfection adds an interesting eccentricity to the room.

Colors appear differently from room to room, city to country, and under different lighting. You would be astonished at how fresh and bright colors look in California. A clear white linen in Los Angeles can appear grayish, positively dull and drab in New York, just as the same shade in Manhattan seems transformed in London. Light changes in

each hemisphere and with every new season. Similarly, colors that are elegant and sophisticated in an urban environment can sometimes look cold, formidable, and uninviting in the suburbs or the country.

As an exercise in seeing, try to spend an entire day looking at colors. In mid-March I visited my friend Ezra's farm in Santa Ynez, an area of glorious mountains and farmlands a short drive north of Santa Barbara. I love thinking about color in this type of setting. On my drive up to the farm I was awed, as always, by the rock formations and the murky, burnished green brush that surrounded them, with many shades of smoky gray, dry clay brown, and a special soft melon green. I have seen many mountain settings, but the light that day played with the colors of the land in a particularly potent way to create stunningly subtle variations I have never experienced before.

An old circular staircase I found in the Paris flea market has been reinforced to reach the sleeping alcove in my studio.

I was eager to create an entire room using those musty tones. At the moment I am trying to recapture them and the sensations I felt on the drive, but this is not quite so simple. What I recall from the car ride is a wish to use many shades of gray and dry, earthy brown together, with that tentative, fresh honeydew-melon green.

Another quirky thing happened that weekend. On Monday morning, I looked out the window on a gray, cloudy day. It had rained heavily all night. The grassy slopes behind the farm, framed by my window, were in focus, as if I were seeing them through a camera lens. They were alive with cows—black-and-white cows, brown-and-white cows, plain white cows, cows everywhere. I felt that I was back in Ireland again, watching the cows strung along the shamrock hills of Shannon. Here, they were surrounded by a backdrop of inky gray-blue sky as they grazed on clear, bright green spring grass. A picture came to my mind of a modern white room with tobacco leather chairs, pale palomino-colored upholstery, black-and-white and pale-brown-and-white cowhides on a stone floor, and that clear bright grass-green color as an accent on pillows. The wetness of the morning evoked the feeling of glass and steel, and I envisioned the slate floors as a pale, rainy-day sort of tinselly gray, with some perfectly simple pieces of sky blue and soft green early Chinese porcelain resting on a table of clear glass and steel.

We had an enormous country breakfast that morning with eggs so freshly laid that they were still warm when they were brought into the kitchen. The color of their yolks was extremely strong, a shade worthy of being remembered, yellow with a tiny drop of orange, a rich and wonderful marmalade sort of color offset by the many grays of the dull day. With our eggs, we had freshly baked bread with white Greek cheese and delicious homemade bitter grape jam, which immediately brought to mind visions of a color scheme of mushroom gray with accents of vivid yellow, white milk paint on the walls, and purplish grape accents.

It was early in the morning and the fire was blazing. Few things are more luxurious than a fire during breakfast—always brilliant on brisk weekend mornings. We were obviously not eager to leave the warm farmhouse for the long ride home, so I purposely took my time. While everyone was finishing the last of their coffee, an amazing thing happened: it began to snow. Soft, haphazard white flakes so large that they looked like Hollywood fakes. Snow in California! In March! Reluctantly, I went back to my room to gather my books and bags and start the journey home. I looked out the window to see how the cows were faring in the snow, but they had all disappeared. Then I did a double take, for there was a large brown creature in the middle of the far end of the field, resting, oblivious to the white flakes around him, motionless as a statue, looking straight ahead.

It was not a mirage. I ran into the kitchen to tell everybody that there was a strange animal sitting on the grass outside my window. It turned out to be a llama originally imported from Peru. It seems llamas are a useful addition to any farm, chomping on the fields of grass in such a way that mowing and clipping are not needed. The creature was a truly surreal sight sitting on the bright grass with the white flakes dropping densely around him, and my mind turned to what I could create with these colors. Perhaps a room in a traditional context, with light, llama-colored walls, a deep shade of honey on the upholstery, a touch of snowy-white taffeta on some soft pillows, pale driftwood-gray wood floors, a piece or two of furniture in a dry white wood-chipped finish, with accents the aqua of the snow-softened sky.

That same weekend I'd caught sight of a rooster in the road at the farm, and his colors had reminded me of the apartment I'd described earlier with the winding hallway, for his feathers were different shades of

Color can be introduced tem-
porarily or permanently,
in subtle or bold ways, to any
setting. Here, the green of
the flowers, the ivory handles
of antique silverware and
the old majolica, and the
introduction of a vivid
blue create a fresh feeling
for entertaining. Collecting
unusual tableware is a rewarding and practical pastime.

tobacco, pale toast, and a tiny bit of bright white, while his rubbery headdress was a florid, bright orange-red. While I certainly would have noticed the brilliant color possibilities in the rooster, I probably would never have made the connection if I had not been writing about the cinnabar hallway. Nature provides inspiration always, but our pleasure in visual beauty gives us the impetus to create.

When choosing fabrics, wall colors, wallpapers, or carpets, always be aware of the differences in texture. They are present in a smooth, flat wall color, a low, lush carpet, sumptuous and sensual velvet, the soft, articulated bumpiness of ribbed corduroy, sleek silk, polished leather, luxurious wool cashmere, fuzzy mohair, waxed and glowing wood, crackled lacquer, cold stone, and crispy, crunchable taffeta. Fabrics and materials are not inanimate; they possess highly individual qualities that create visual and sensual dimensions.

Try to arrange all your materials so you can study them together. Are there too many fabrics with a similar texture—maybe mohair, velvet, corduroy, wool? Do these materials feel too much alike? If so, remove what you can part with and add a few materials that have a different feel —perhaps fresh, crisp linen, needlepoint, textured straw, suede, wood, slick steel, or rough grosgrain. Add lots of contrasts, not necessarily in color but in quality and touch. Mohair feels and looks soft and warm, for example, while marble brings in a cool, hard surface. Silk is flimsy and feminine, while leather is firm, tight, and masculine. Contrasts work off each other: stone and wood, straw and glass. We could play this game for hours.

You may choose to use one predominant color in a room, but it is in adding many different textures and surfaces that you will keep it from becoming tiresome. Gazing out the window this instant, I notice the different textures in the garden: branches, earth, stone, sky, and an infinite tapestry of green, from moss to kelly; the sheer variety keeps me absorbed. Consider this: when people dismiss a beige room, perhaps this is because it is simply beige and boring. Maybe the artist—and let us use this term for anyone who is creating his or her own space—has been unable to create visual and tactile vitality. If we are conscious of how to use form, proportion, and shape to define a room, we may sometimes believe that changing the shapes and sizes of our furniture will create all the interest needed. Not so. Every variation in texture will bring added interest: the smooth, dull glow of a worn brass fireplace implement, or the natural straw weave of a tiny basket holding fine, softly starched linen napkins on the waxed surface of a lovely old table. Each textured element resonates in a different way, creating a symphony of contrasts, a kind of discord that adds vigor and inevitably creates a harmony that the eye and the soul can be at peace with.

My boarding-school days influenced my design aesthetic profoundly. Rose Haven School for Girls was a highly structured environment. Each morning we would find a wicker basket sitting at the foot of our beds containing clean, name-tagged underwear and a neatly folded uniform. The system was not perfect; there were times when a small girl would appear at breakfast with bloomers down to her knees, and an older one would be wearing a jumper that ended somewhere just below her waist. Wrong basket!

It was there at Rose Haven that I began to appreciate certain textures and shapes and shades of color. We were all assigned chores to do on Saturday mornings. One of these was to wax the furniture, including that in the dining room—large, round, wooden tables and small Windsor chairs, all in dark, well-polished wood. In the whitewashed sleeping rooms were rows of small, wooden beds, each covered with pure white, cotton sheets and well-washed wool blankets of a deep cream. Everything was immaculately clean and fresh, with no other tones except white and cream next to the dark, highly polished wood floors; there was absolutely no ornamentation whatsoever. As you can see from my work, the combination of good woods and simple furniture has been the foundation of my design sensibility ever since.

At Rose Haven, color came as a reward. If we made an excellent grade in certain classes we were allowed the treat of selecting pansies to plant in our own small garden patch. I was very discriminating about what colors to choose for my tiny garden, and the colors in pansies still fascinate me today—the way the browns are almost claret colored and how, when the velvety-brown graduates into yellow, there is the thin line of purple.

The lesson to be learned from flowers is that few colors do not work well together if the right shade is used. Again look at the colors you are considering at different times of the day, in different lights, and in the space in which they will eventually be placed. The same color will change completely at different times of the day or night according to the reflectivity of the surface. But in choosing a palette, it will be helpful if you first select the basic background hues for the walls, floors, and window treatments. Then consider introducing the accent colors in art, accessories, carpets, and objects. It is exhilarating to use colors that are conventionally considered odd together, or to combine certain colors in a totally unexpected way. One of my favorite rooms is a great hall in England where the walls are white and the floors and paneling are dark oak. Covering the dark Jacobean period furniture is fabric of the most delicate powder pink. When I first saw this hall, I caught my breath, for it was as unexpected as it was beautiful. What was especially fascinating

The way the light enters and is experienced in the living room of a Richard Meier house in Malibu is the result of pure architectural magic in collaboration with nature.

Furnishing this beach house was not unlike attempting to arrange areas of comfortable living space inside a large piece of superb sculpture.

was the fact that the fabric covering this imposing furniture was not the heavy brocade or cut velvet that the period called for, and that one would expect in a great hall. Instead, it was a pale pink muslin, a simple, uncomplicated, humble fabric. What is usually considered a nursery color was added quite felicitously to this austere and masculine room.

Had I been the designer of that hall, I probably would have found myself using, much less successfully, a bolder palette. How I wished I would have had the inspiration to use that perfect pale pink!

Color is especially wonderful in bedrooms, where you might fill the entire room with color. In the main living areas, you may limit yourself to smaller doses of interchangeable color. We tire less quickly of colors in the bedroom than if those same colors were used in the living room. If what you see from your window is a garden, the sea, or glorious mountains, do not try to compete with nature. If you are fortunate enough to have such a view, you have the opportunity to harmonize your room with the outdoors so that the two become an extension of each other. In a beach house in construction at the moment where Richard Meier is the architect (not the one depicted in the photos here), we are choosing fabrics for the furniture in the shades of the ocean water, which can be seen from every room. In the summer, the water is many silvery shades of a soft aquamarine; in the colder months, it is a moody, muddy mixture of gray, greens, and gray-blue. In choosing colors, I tried to imagine how the room would look if it were a raft drifting in the water. Would you use light, watery, misty gray-blues for the coverings of the furniture? The floors will be a driftwood dry clay shade, which is an extension of the surrounding teak patios. Nature and man; where one ends, the other begins. There is an exquisite feeling of light and peace when this is accomplished.

Decorators often speak of the no-color room, but the term is misleading. There is no such thing as a colorless room, just as there are no such persons as colorless people. The poet William Carlos Williams said, "Nothing is as white as the memory of white." In my living room, for example, you can count the many shades of white. (An irate neighbor who was becoming weary of my workmen parking too near her house when we were under construction wrote me a charming but agitated note, addressing me as "Dear owner of the Vanilla Villa.") Even before the furniture was installed, the natural plaster pigment of the rooms had turned a parchment color, which seemed to permeate the space. If you were here you would agree that to say that the room is colorless is far from accurate: color abounds in the dark wood ceiling and the waxed wood floors, the many shades of the antique wood furniture, the hundreds of hues of the book bindings, the different worn leathers, heavy hemps, and flax that cover various chairs, the faded velvet sofas, the deep tones of the ivory keys on the spinet piano, the intricate straw American Indian baskets, the muted celadon color in the Chinese porcelain, the glow of the bronze sculpture, the many shadings in the stone of the mantels and creamy color of the rugs, the worn, rich green velvet pillows, the pencil drawings and ink sketches, the opalescent blue-green of the Roman glass, the vivid green of the garden outside framed by the wooden doors, the color and texture of the delicate vines that have invited themselves indoors as permanent guests enveloping and etching my walls with their lacy leaves, the clear cobalt and white sky that is visible from my chair, the glow of flames in the hearth—on and on and on.

It is a Sunday afternoon in April and I have been writing in the garden for the past few hours. The sun is setting and the beauty of the room is now found in the shadows, in the pools of darkness that fall in wells in the corners and leave just a small section of the room highlighted. The many shades of the setting sun enter only tentatively, as if they fear to be diminished by the shadows and faded into nothingness. Wait: now the sunset does disappear, leaving a jagged line of vivid lavender in its wake. It too fades; left are only the shadows and the flickering amber flame from the hearth. To turn on a light would be a harsh intrusion, so let us just sit here for a moment longer, remembering the light.

It is hard to discuss color without beginning with blue. Along with green, blue surrounds us everywhere, every day of our lives. Any shade of blue is brilliant with any shade of white, as well as with any shade of green—chartreuse, apple, moss, celadon, or hunter. Though I like almost all blues, I tend to be drawn to two shades in particular: Prussian blue (a pigment discovered in the 1700s) and indigo blue. Indigo blue has a gray cast, while Prussian blue has a very slight green cast. This green blue is a wonderful color to use anywhere, as it has a rich, vibrant quality. Think of it as the perfect accent for a room filled with neutral shades of toast, cordovan, and caramel.

As you can see from the photos on pages 64 and 109 I have been very influenced by my visit to Ireland. I have been using a fresh, clear green that is not quite a garden variety but that has a touch of sapphire in it, a slightly lighter shade than kelly. You can sometimes find pieces of painted American furniture in this color. Celadon is a color that can be used quite easily; I collect early pottery in this muted and sometimes murky shade. Isn't it true that the green of trees nurtures the soul in a special way? Imagine a sunporch filled with dark forest green wicker furniture and lots of white. And why not a crisp celery-green room? Thinking in color has the power to contradict any too rapid proclamation one might make.

Tangerine, melon, flame, and amber are colors that glow wherever they go. Years ago, I designed a guest room for a client in a deep, rich canteloupe melon color combined with accents of clear, sharp vermilion. The woodwork was a bright white, and all the walls were covered in a melon-colored fabric that had a small red chinoiserie pattern on it. A few chairs were covered in deep coral gros point, and there was lots of black lacquer about. The minute you stepped into that room you felt all aglow and quite happy to be there.

Purple is the color of passion. You either love it or you passionately do not want to live with it. For years I have been buying from a fabric shop in Rome called Lisio, a small store filled with shelves of samples, from which you place an order. For as long as I could remember, instead of doors, a double pair of portieres partitioned off the back room from the shop. The portieres were of heavy, rich, dark purple silk

RIGHT) The juxtaposition of dark woods, light walls, and vivid color make this corner of a pool house kitchen a treat for the eye. OVERLEAF) The worn silk velvet on this amazing Georgian chair is the most perfect purple. I found the fabric hanging as a pair of portieres in a shop in Rome and covered several pieces of furniture with it. The chair is placed in front of a desk table by the window of a dining room–library, a cozy corner for tête-à-tête dining.

velvet, the quality of which you could never duplicate today, for they were woven on very narrow ancient looms, of the finest threads of silk you can imagine. I have rarely seen such beautiful velvet. Over the years, the shop owner became a friend, and for ages I hinted that I would love to purchase the purple portieres. One day we were having coffee, the best coffee in the world at St. Estauch, my favorite coffee bar in Rome. After our third espresso, Signore Frasca announced that he was at last willing to part with the velvet portieres. The fabric now covers a few very fine antique pieces in a client's paneled library–dining room. Worn and faded, the velvet is still glorious.

Purple will always be the color associated in my mind with Rose Cummings, in her time a formidable antiques dealer and design innovator—Rose, with the amethyst hair. As a young design student, I was asked to spend time at a fabric house, an auction gallery, or an antiques shop, and then to write a paper about the experience. I chose the Rose Cummings shop and was granted permission by Miss Cummings's sister, Eileen (I too have a sister Eileen), to visit and spend time there. I wish you could have seen that shop. It was quite simply like stepping into another world. The large open space had high ceilings and oddly placed, old panels of worn *boiserie*; a glass menagerie of magnificent chandeliers hung everywhere; and wonderful faded and threadbare silk fabrics covered the over- and underscaled furniture. The pieces in that shop had personalities so strong that you knew you would rarely encounter such animated souls again. There were silver stools, the finish all but flaked off, with torn and worn gorgeous velvet hanging off them. The entire room was filled with an un-self-conscious style that had been created by this strong, eccentric woman over many years. From the moment I entered that shop I knew I too wanted to be a shopkeeper—to deal in antiques, and to surround myself with beautiful things.

Confessions of a Shopkeeper

One of my great challenges in life is controlling the temptation to purchase everything I fall in love with. Once I discover a treasure, I am compelled to find it a home.

A few years ago, while helping a client put together a collection of antiques during a trip to Europe, I found a very fine William and Mary chest on a stand that I wanted her to consider. An admirably practical woman, she agreed that it was a marvelous piece, but not something we had planned for. Did we really have a place for it? It was an absolutely relevant question, so I proposed a compromise. If I could suggest two places where it would work, would she feel comfortable enough to buy it? She agreed, I specified the possible locations, we bought the piece, and ultimately her designer used it in an entirely different and more prominent location than I had suggested. The point of the story is that if you find something you feel passionately about, you will find a place for it. So whenever you consider a piece of furniture or an object that you had not proposed in your original plan, try to envision several areas where you are confident it would work comfortably.

I have been fortunate that my work has provided an outlet for my obsession with finding and buying wonderful antiques. Whether it is for my home, my shop, a client, or another designer, the thrill is in both finding *and* obtaining.

Before acquiring, of course, should come knowing. I once thought of writing a book about antiques and calling it *Louis Seize What?* While a large and important part of the knowledge of antique furniture and objects can be taught in the classroom, there is much to be learned in the field. The history of the decorative arts is fascinating, and studying the evolution of furniture and architecture is vitally important for the student of design. A student can gather all the information needed to identify a certain piece of furniture, yet still be caught short when taken to the school of surprises: the auction rooms. It is here that one must acquire a sense of how to appraise furniture and objects—not only from the exquisite renderings in books but from the existing examples actually available. So the education of a student of furniture will never be complete without intensive field study. A piece must be thoroughly examined if one is to understand all there is to know about it.

My own education was further encouraged by the marvelous antiques dealers I met when I first began my career. One dealer I had the privilege of knowing was the late Monsieur Litbury, who had a superb shop on the Left Bank in Paris. White-haired, very tall, extremely handsome, and truly elegant (like most dealers), he had a great appreciation for all the pieces in his shop. As I examined an object he would point out, sometimes in French and sometimes in broken English, that it had never been restored, saying, *"Pas touché; virgin."* He would open every door, pull out every drawer, and turn each piece over to point with pride at

his *never-been-touched* furniture. He would hold his nose close to it, breathe in its aroma, and heave a sigh of pure pleasure, as if he were savoring the full body of a fine wine. He could determine the age of a piece by the dryness of its wood and the nuances of its aroma—he knew not only the age of a piece but its true essence.

In educating oneself in the different periods of furniture, one discovers each has its own special idiosyncracies by which it is defined. For example, the quiet elegance of the furniture of the Queen Anne period is visible in its pier mirrors, which are simple and graceful, and in its chairs and cabinets. At that time, Asian exports were continually flowing into England through the British East India Company, and into France through the Campagnie des Indes under the auspices of Madame de Pompadour. The chinoiserie wallpapers and lacquer furniture that

A doorway in a client's master bedroom. On either side stand a pair of wonderful antique English cabinets.

LEFT) I cannot resist any type of bookshelf or book rest. The narrow chair is amusing and eccentric. BELOW) Régence chairs covered in their original Beauvais tapestry add pattern and texture to this room. The Chinese antique lacquer table is piled with books and a few American Indian baskets. The chair in the back, one of a pair, is Georgian, and the fraying skin is its original covering.

emerged in the Queen Anne period are some of the very best pieces in the history of furniture.

Georgian furniture is stronger and more heavily carved than its Queen Anne precedents. The glorious pieces of William Kent are from this period, as is the furniture by Thomas Chippendale, who refined the existing furniture styles in every way. Chippendale's designs were inspired by many sources: classic Italian art, Gothic tracery, Chinese latticework and bamboo, and many French forms. Some of his best work was designed in collaboration with the Scottish architect and designer Robert Adam. It was also during these years of the mid–eighteenth century that there was a revival in England of the Gothic forms; instead of the heavy oak of the Gothic period in room designs, however, delicate pine was often substituted. At Strawberry Hill, the estate of the great Georgian diarist Horace Walpole, neo-Gothic architecture found its most exciting expression. The photograph on page 232 shows a room of paneling purported to have been purchased from Strawberry Hill. Transplanted, it is as beautiful as it is whimsical.

When I first opened my antiques shop, at times a client would come in and assume that I was an employee. If I sensed that he or she might feel more comfortable with this assumption, I would keep my proprietorship to myself. I was in my twenties, and while my youth did not always work to my disadvantage, I have since learned that wisdom often does come with age. At first, certain dealers and shopkeepers in Europe did not take me as seriously as I would have wished, though this was not long the case, for once dealers knew me as a serious student, their attitude changed. All antiques traders and shopkeepers are students, as daily there is something new that must be learned.

In those early years I was consumed by my interest in Chinese porcelain and carried a collection of both early pottery and Chinese export in my shop. (In England, many of the collectors in this particular field sell privately, either from their homes or by appointment.) As I made the rounds of dealers in the months when I was still building my reputation and inventory, I repeatedly encountered a certain tall, elderly gentleman. He had stooped shoulders and white, rather long hair; he wore a long, rumpled raincoat and an odd floppy, old felt hat. He carried a mysterious large canvas bag. I observed that every time he inspected a piece, he would whip out a magnifying glass and study it carefully. All the dealers seemed inordinately attentive to him, while I, on the other hand, was totally ignored. I tried to study his technique. One day I saw him lift a small Korean pottery bowl above his head and run his tongue over the bottom edge. Why was he doing this? While many early Korean pieces are often unglazed at the bottom edge and slightly rough to the touch, it does not take a tongue to discover this. In any case, I was deeply impressed by this gesture, for it looked terribly professional, and I decided to try it in the next shop I visited, hoping I would look as knowledgeable; perhaps then I would be taken seriously. At the next opportunity, I lifted a similar piece of porcelain to my mouth and slowly, sensuously ran my tongue around the bottom as I had seen the old sage do. The shopkeeper looked at me rather strangely and then came up to me and asked with some concern if something was wrong. I felt an utter fool, which of course I was. Maybe the old man knew I was studying him and did this simply to confuse me. To this day, knowing all that I now know, I still have no idea what he gained by licking that bowl. The lesson here: suppress the need to impress.

An antiques dealer's life is almost as difficult as it is blissful. It is a passionate life that constantly demands new fulfillment. All the profit you make is continually in use, buying ever more merchandise. It is an end-

120

PRECEDING PAGE) An English Regency cupboard holds a collection of antique ivory carved fruits and objects. The doors of the cupboard wrap around to close it off, which makes the piece very unusual. ABOVE) An eighteenth-century artist's mannequin sits in front of architectural elements and a very fine seventeenth-century Chinese watercolor of silverfish. LEFT) Arranging objects and collections on tables can create a very personal collage. Here is a small carved antique box in the shape of a foot, next to Japanese ink pots that rest on a worn American Indian mat.

less circle: you sell and then try to replace, and each replacement becomes more costly. Yet the most joy-filled days of my working life were when I dealt exclusively in antiques.

In those early years, before I went to Paris to buy, for months I would set aside the money I earned in the shop. As soon as I arrived home, I would anxiously await the time I could return to buy again. And while I was there, the pressure was always fierce.

The French love to argue and discuss everything in depth. Selling a piece of furniture is no fun for most French dealers unless they can get in some solid hours of intense negotiating, which can be a great waste of time for buyers on a schedule. One dealer, Madame Manon, had a shop of four floors stocked with furniture and objects. She was an excellent dealer with a strict rule: no negotiating. She would state her price and then just stand there, her cigarette dangling from her mouth, saying nothing. She had not one ounce of charm, but I always felt better after dealing with her, because I knew that no other buyer would be treated differently, even if her mood changed. And nobody's time was wasted. I once saw her in the street and did not recognize her, because in her shop she seemed so formidable, and here she looked like an ordinary mortal; she was also without the Gauloise cigarette that was usually glued to her lower lip.

One tremendous reward of those difficult days was that I learned that negotiating is an art all its own. I came to understand that it is imperative never to criticize a dealer's piece or its price. Praise it for its perfection, even though it may have a few problems that you could easily pick on; nothing is more annoying than a potential buyer's finding fault with the stock the shopkeeper has selected.

One of my most amusing lessons in how *not* to negotiate came from a friend who was selling a set of forty antique Chinese-export dinner dishes in his shop. The price he was asking was equal to the value of the plates, and they were in quite excellent condition. A prospective buyer negotiated the price with him for ages and kept denigrating each piece, saying she had seen the same period Chinese export plates for a bit less somewhere else. The dealer was becoming increasingly annoyed and finally said to her, "Madame, just what would it make you happy to pay?" Very pleased with her negotiating acumen, she named her paltry price. With a benign smile on his face, the dealer picked up the dishes, lifted them high in the air, and, with perfect precision, dropped the whole stack on the floor, smashing them to smithereens. "Now, Madame, you can have them for that amount," he said. The horrified look on the buyer's face, he later told me, was payment enough for him.

I opened Tarlow Antiques in 1976; I was in my twenties, and this was my first serious antiques shop. I had found the most ideal location imaginable on Melrose Place in Los Angeles, right next door to where my present shop is. Before the opening, I went off to buy in Europe with what today would not be enough money for one Regency chair, determined to choose pieces that I felt would constitute a unique selection. I looked only for very special things, each with a personality of its own. I tried to keep in mind the advice of Louis C. Tiffany, who said, "Never buy what you think will sell, only things you would want for yourself," a piece of wisdom that I still practice. Even if I could sell hundreds of a certain piece, if it was not the quality I wanted to represent my shop, I would not consider buying it. Similarly, you should never put anything in your house unless you feel that you absolutely have to have it.

The night before the opening of my shop, everything was still in chaos and there were only three of us to prepare for the next day, which I was dreading. My husband and Diego, the furniture polisher who still works in my shop, and I pushed furniture around for hours. It was one in the morning when we all finally left, exhausted. I was in tears and totally discouraged. Just a few weeks before, innocent and eager, I had stood under an umbrella in the rain at four in the morning at the Paris flea markets, only to find that nobody would appear for hours. Now, on the night before opening my shop, I was tired and weary of the whole notion of antiques. How could I have ever imagined that I could accomplish this? At that moment I wanted to hide in my house forever, but at dawn the next morning we were back at work in what still looked like a dreary room, the windows papered up and the furniture and accessories crammed and jammed into the center.

We worked without resting, pushing and moving things into place, and within the next few hours everything just came together. It was as if a miracle had taken place.

It was a small shop with a private center garden courtyard that you

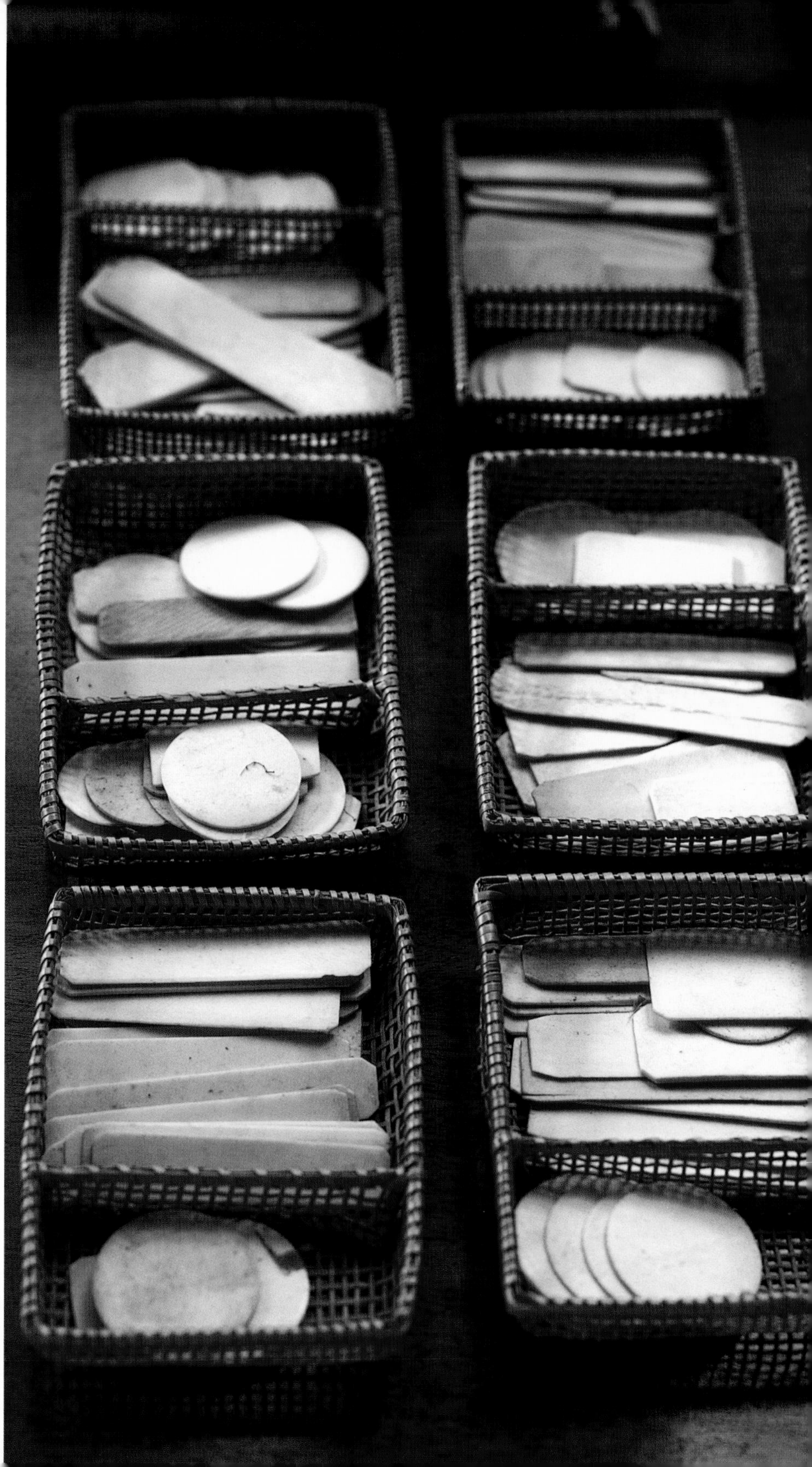

The ivory disks came from an old game box, from which I removed the colored disks and kept the ivory ones. The baskets are so intricately and beautifully woven that the paper-thin geometric pieces have become exquisite objects of art within them.

could glimpse as you walked in the door. By the time the doors opened that morning, visitors entered to see a massive eighteenth-century French stone table in the middle of the room, on top of which was an enormous antique wire birdcage filled with hundreds of tiny, brightly colored birds. The furniture and the floors had been waxed till they glowed. A fire was burning in the stone fireplace. Outside, I had filled the patio with white flowering trees, and the sun was shining. The fascinating thing about that day was that I did not feel for one minute that I was the one who had created this. It was as if someone else had taken over, someone who knew exactly what had to be done. I began to understand that while magic may not always arrive the second I wish for it, it will happen.

Today, I may be working on a prototype of a piece of furniture and feel uninspired about its design. But I have developed enough confidence in my judgment that I am able to move on, expecting that the next time I come back to it, I will recognize every flaw and know immediately what to do.

When you are working on your own house and feel equally uninspired, stop for a while; let it go. Look through a book on design that might give you inspiration, or maybe read a book that has nothing to do with design. Sometimes trying too hard to make the right decision leads us to make either the wrong one or one that is far too contrived.

Having a room respond to your vision is like filling in a preliminary sketch. Sometimes it is necessary to spend hours rearranging rugs, accessories, furniture, or simply a corner of the room; at other times the settling in may take only a moment. In a painting, even the slightest brushstroke can have the power to change awkwardness into perfection. This process is an expected element in creativity.

Here, a collection of old English pewter chargers, treen plates, and a lingam vessel filled with rare painted tole leaves are placed near a set of 1920s French porcelain dishes. The plates inspired me in the design of my own dishware.

A Window Outside

Do you remember how as a child the light from the hallway could be seen under the door of your bedroom, giving you a feeling of comfort and safety? Light is so enormously potent and evocative that it is not surprising that many religious cultures have referred to their all-powerful deity as the Light. No matter what we call the phenomenon that illuminates our lives, it has the power to invade or enhance, to coldly expose, to softly blend or warmly dramatize.

Light is the most intellectually challenging element of nature and is probably most deeply appreciated by those who have to use it to its best advantage, especially farmers, scientists, and master builders. It is not by chance that a ray of sunlight through a cathedral window enters in such a way that it has the power to lift us to another realm. As we create and design the lighting in our lives, we are engaging in addressing its quality, its color, its direction and intensity, how well it helps us to see, and how it makes us feel. It is a never-ending consideration.

Each season offers us distinctly varied emotions, partly because of the particular nature of its light.

SPRING: CALIFORNIA. It is noon and the light is directly overhead and quite intense, charged with the vitality that comes in spring. The leaves in the trees are filmy and bright. Within weeks, they will toughen in texture and darken, losing their vivid color. We have planted hundreds of tiny purple crocuses all over the lawn, hoping that they will bloom when the wisteria covers the house and the lavender appears. Imagine purple everywhere! Nature is fraught with expectation in the crisp spring light.

SUMMER: PROVENCE. We take a drive south for the day and arrive in time to have lunch by the sea. The sunlight dances and sparkles on the surface of the water as we sit at our table, drinking a light rosé, which never tastes as divine anywhere else. We are enjoying a deliciously long lunch. The midday light in summer is potent and steamy, the sun's rays dancing on the water. The sun's warmth bathes our bare arms.

AUTUMN: LONG ISLAND. The light is at its most dramatic and mellow in September. The trees are glorious this autumn, with leaves of pink, peach, mauve, burgundy, and soft yellow—a very different palette than what I assume autumn colors to be: rust, red, gold, and burnished brown. The autumn air is heavy and pungent with the small of decaying leaves, while the light is soft and dreamlike, neither as bold and clear as in the spring, nor as sharp and penetrating as in winter.

Autumn light is a flattering light—tender, delicate, and softly glowing. Lost is the bright, hot arrogance of spring and summer. In autumn, light becomes softened and mellowed around the edges. Autumn light, for all its intensity of glorious color, has a melancholy tinge to it.

WINTER: MANHATTAN. Curled up, warm and cozy by a window in a comfortable chair, I look out at the snow that has fallen heavily during the

My pool sits on a hillside and is completely secluded from everything but nature. The old tiles were imported from England with the moss still on them.

K. MALEVICH
SUPREMATISM
P. RAILING
The Graphic Art of Winslow Homer
NCENT VAN GOGH
LEONARDO DA VINCI
AUGUSTE RENOIR
LEONARDO DA VINCI

A collection of architecture
books is framed in a doorway
into the garden.

night. The white, wet powder covers everything in sight. Touched by the wintry light, it glitters as if the earth has been sprinkled with tiny faceted diamonds. It is February and last night's snowstorm has made New York a wonderland. We are on the north side of this apartment building in a room that usually has a soft, even light, but the reflection of the sun on the snow-covered roof across the way has made it dazzlingly bright; sunglasses are in order.

Think of how light can be reflected, in this instance in a room facing north. The white of the snow acted as a recipient for the sunlight and reflected it into the otherwise quite dark little room. My son Glen's apartment in New York faces north, and as an artist he quite likes it. He says, however, that at a specific time every day the sun bounces its rays off a white building up the block from him and floods his rooms with light for a short time. You can mimic this effect by using mirrors to bring light into an area that otherwise is without it.

Artists prefer the light of a northern exposure because it is relatively stable and allows color to be accurately portrayed. Halogen light is the artificial counterpart of northern light since it is a whiter light that is excellent for illuminating art and capturing true color. South or southwest light is not as even or predictable: it has a sunny cast, an incandescent, golden glow that is much like that provided by an incandescent tungsten bulb.

The earliest and most primitive light sources were the Sun and the illumination of fires. Sun and fire still perform the same vital tasks for us today but are generally taken for granted now that light can be manipulated and moved about at will. Light can be retracted, diffused, or directed with a flick of a switch or a twist of that brilliant invention, the dimmer. The power to create many different sensations is available: it can be serene or flamboyant, petulant or moody. We have the choice of using light that is hot or cold, soft or hard. Once it has been adjusted to suit each season, light can be fixed the way we wish it to be and will then remain fairly predictable in the future.

Rooms facing east will receive the morning sun, and those facing west will have sun in the afternoon; this is a consideration in deciding which way to site a new house, or when purchasing an existing one. If it is your pleasure to wake up in a light, bright room, you may want to face your bedroom to the east. In the warm months, the best place to dine is in a room that faces west, as the sun sets there, whereas rooms facing south will have light all day long. I discovered an interesting problem with siting when looking at ancient houses in Provence. They were situated in a way that protected them from both the heat of the day and the fierce winds of the mistral. This led to houses that we would consider dark and gloomy because of the lack of windows but that in pre-electric days were cool in summer and snug in winter.

Today we can choose where and when the property will receive light. An eastern exposure in the kitchen is delightful, for having breakfast in a room flooded with sunlight is a splendid way to begin the day, while the daytime rooms that face west receive the most substantial light later. The ideal solution is to have more than one exposure in a room.

If we can harness light by calibrating its location, it will reward us by gracing our lives. From the very outset of designing any space, ask yourself: Where are the windows placed? Are they the right size? Is it necessary to add more windows? Is it possible to change windows into French doors to allow more light into this space? Should skylights be considered? How will the light fall, at what angle, and at what time of day? Is there something to see through the windows that will augment the beauty of this room? If the view is unrewarding, would it be best to create a more introverted space?

I was recently in a Manhattan apartment visiting a new friend for lunch. When I entered her living room, I immediately saw bright red walls—not the burnished red usually favored but a clean, hot, fresh, fire-engine red. Everything in the room was bright. Some paintings were abstract works, some not. The sofas and comfortable club chairs were all covered in a floral chintz with a white background and clear colors. The decorations on the unlit Christmas tree were bright balls of glowing color. Indeed, color was everywhere you looked, refreshing and stimulating: the room sang and invited you to join in. We went into the kitchen and again, another surprise: the kitchen was flooded with natural light—strong, southern light that would keep it bright and light throughout the day. Until that moment one would not have realized that the living room had a northern exposure, or that it was the darker room. That bright clear red had the power to create and reflect its own light and lift the spirits of anyone who entered the room.

If eyes are the windows to our souls, then windows are the eyes into the soul of a house. Biking into the village of East Hampton recently a friend and I pedaled by a large construction site. "Do you want to stop for a minute to look?" my friend asked. "Why?" was my quick response. At a glance, we could spot five different windowpane sizes in the house's many randomly placed windows. Just looking in their direction could cause you to lose your equilibrium and fall off your bike—as I nearly did—with the urge to mentally rearrange the disorderly and agitated state of the design.

Symmetry brings harmony into our lives. To this end, I am constantly urging students and clients to make doors and windows symmetrical, for this establishes balance and delivers an immediate sense of order and integrity to an architectural concept. It's an important ingredient to the ultimate success of a beautiful space.

Harmony and balance on the exterior of a house are as important as

RIGHT) I like to imagine that Keats or Shelley could have used this iron-and-leather lectern to read his works to an audience. BELOW) An eighteenth-century French settee that opens into a bed was probably one of the earliest predecessors to today's Hide-A-Bed. An antique textile is wrapped around its pullout canopy.

balance on a bike: one false shift in position and you are flat on your fanny. Careful planning should therefore precede any new construction to ensure the symmetry and proportion that are indispensable to the success of traditional architecture. Exterior symmetry in window placement is as important as interior symmetry in furniture placement; whatever is added or subtracted should be of the same material and entirely sympathetic with the integrity of the structure.

Windows—their placement, number and size—are the first source of light to consider. Equally important are the design and placement of electrical lighting. Once you know approximately the size and position of the rugs to be used in a room, you can address the issue of artificial lighting and electrical outlets. The expression *plug-ugly* may not have originated this way, but it's a good reminder: plugs and outlets are like blemishes on walls, so place them as discreetly as possible.

Using your floor plan, establish a clear idea of where table lamps are to be situated; then outlets can easily be installed in the floor beneath them, and long, trippy cords can be eliminated. Arrange to put wall outlets and phone plugs near base moldings, where they are accessible but barely visible, and on the floor under the sofa or main seating. A floor plan is indispensable for providing such unfortunate necessities as outlets for your lamps, whereas overhead light will be designed to fall from chandeliers, recessed lights, or carefully placed spotlights. I have a special aversion to seeing multiple intrusions on a ceiling. Overhead lights can cast brutal shadows on the faces of those poor unfortunates sitting beneath them and turn a handsome prince back into a frog.

When freshening up a tired room, try removing the curtains from your windows to find a lighter, more contemporary way of filtering the light. Windows are like paintings in a room: what they frame can be as beautiful and interesting as any piece of art, and oftentimes is more so.

Many bedrooms need curtains to keep the light out in the morning. But other than here and in media screening rooms, why keep light from entering a room?

I did not use curtains on the windows in this Georgian-style house, deciding instead to create a less formal, more contemporary feeling. In place of the traditional curtains and valances in all the sitting and dining rooms, are simple, light, delicate slat shades made of the same wood and color hue as the pine paneling. The thin wooden slats permit a view of all that is outside while they soften any glare that might otherwise wash out the room and its art. The outcome is exactly what was hoped for; there is now a wonderful sense of unity and harmony between the rooms, which did not exist before, and the house feels fresh and young, flooded with a soft, mellow light from dawn to dusk. "The better the room, the less need for curtains," wrote Edith Wharton and Ogden Codman in *The Decoration of Houses.*

Whereas insufficient light in a room can be oppressive, a great deal of light is not always flattering to its occupants or its furnishings. But between the two, an overabundance of light is preferable, since it can always be manipulated. In my house, the living room has large French doors on both sides, yet the light does not need to be restrained; given the orientation of the house on the property, the trees outside the French doors allow just the right degree of obstructed light to enter the room. Even during the brightest hours of the day, the light is naturally and beautifully filtered by the large pines. If the room gets too shadowy, I know the trees need a clipping.

To avoid a feeling of darkness in a room that does not have a very high ceiling, lamps and wall washers (lights that are overhead on the ceiling but only wash the walls) are usually sufficient. But with the

LEFT) Dark mahogany doors create a screen effect, framing both the living room and the sunroom. RIGHT) The oval forms of the fourth-dynasty Egyptian canopic jars are a subtle reminder of the beauty found in strong, simple design.

eighteen-foot ceiling in my living room, this solution would have been difficult. The first night, we sat in the still fairly empty living room and had a cozy picnic by the fire. The room was underlit because I did not want holes for overhead lighting to cut into my glorious wooden ceiling. As it was, there were dark, sad shadows everywhere, which made the room feel like an old boarding school in Budapest. Obviously, I needed to rethink my lighting scheme.

Fortunately, electricity had been installed just in case it was needed, so it was relatively simple to pull the wires and add light fittings—a precaution that, knowing my penchant for underlighting, I often employ. This solution is not as complicated as it sounds. The wiring is installed where you anticipate additional lighting may one day be needed; then it is plugged up safely and plastered over. If the area does in fact need more overhead light, it is a fairly simple job for the electrician to add new fixtures. Be careful, however, to make careful notes of where the hidden treasure of wires is buried so you don't have to destroy the ceiling if you need additional fixtures.

Harsh, bright lights will wash out and diminish the beauty of even the best art and decoration. For example, having too many recessed lights overhead can destroy a perfectly good ceiling and give any room a disturbingly commercial appearance. While we have rather successfully combated the cottage-cheese ceiling, be aware of the Swiss-cheese ceiling. An abundance of ceiling lights should be limited to kitchens, laundry rooms, and shoe shops.

Modern forms of high-tech lighting can be a refreshing relief from tired old solutions. Some fixtures look positively like sculpture when they are added to a traditionally designed room. On rare occasions use a few uplights or wall washers, but more often, use simple, shaded lamps, with a few ceiling lights cautiously placed in context with the architecture of the room. Remember, the eye travels upward. Ceiling lights that are not based on some sort of symmetrical plan are distracting. And recessed lighting that is not properly lined up or centered on any axis drives me up the wall . . . to rearrange it!

Diverse lighting placed at different levels—high in the ceiling, washing a wall, sitting on tables, cast from floor lamps and from floor uplighting—gives an even, layered look to a room. Near a reading chair, I may use a Hartman lamp, a standing lamp in brass or steel that has a fairly modern metal shield over an angular bulb, casting a small spread of light. Higher light can be created with a pair of lamps on a long table behind a sofa, or on tables on either end of a sofa. A spot in the ceiling could aim its glow on a decorative screen or a piece of sculpture. The ultimate goal, as always, is to create balance and harmony; it is also important to approximate natural light as nearly as possible.

Do be careful in choosing lamp shades. A sea of shades can be overwhelming, especially if they are overscaled. We tend to take lamp shades for granted, but aren't they rather an odd-looking device to put on a lamp? So why enlarge them? Close your eyes and concentrate on the room you are working with, and picture just how many lamp shades will look aesthetically pleasing. If, when you open them again, you see too many shades, then the process of elimination begins with the introduction of other light sources.

Light will fall differently from every type of shade. Vellum shades give a soft, amber glow and are translucent. Opaque paper shades allow the light to flow only from their wide bottom. Silk shades are also translucent but a bit more dressed up than their paper counterparts. In bedrooms, silk shades with small thin pleats are elegant, and give a soft, warm glow to the inhabitants. Years ago, we were taught to line silk shades in a rosy silk to cast an especially flattering and romantic light; it

147

may be time once again for a bit of soft pink light. At a certain age, timing and lighting are everything. Another nice detail for pleated silk shades in the bedroom is to add to the self-silk trim a minuscule line of colored silk cord that ties the shade to the particular color of the lamp base. Lamps can sit on nightstands, or simple swing-arm lamps can be attached to the walls on both sides of larger beds; a single bed may need only one swing-arm lamp. For reading in a bed without a canopy, a small spotlight in the ceiling can be used but, unfortunately, it is not a very flattering light in a bedroom.

It is preferable not to have too many different styles of large shades in any room. I do at times deviate from this, however. At the four corners of my living room are four iron standing lamps whose shades are all square-shaped and made of parchment. These four surfaces of translu-

An antique chair that surely could have inspired the modernist architect and furniture designer Gerrit Reitveld.

cent light give off a balanced, golden glow. In the middle of the room there is a Chinese *blanc de chine* vase with a simple opaque shade that has been painted a hue similar to that of the parchment shades but is of a different shape and material from the others. It exudes its light only from under its shade, so that at night you see the light lingering on the dark wood table that the lamp sits on, but at night the shade itself seems to vanish. It is thus the table that is prominent, not the lamp. This particular lamp sits higher than the other four lamps, which properly disturbs the flat, horizontal mass of the room. The four translucent shades were almost enough for this large room; adding the opaque shade took it to the edge. Again, try and keep the light in the room balanced, to avoid shadowy areas and visual disharmony.

Round diffusers can be placed on top of a shade to keep the light from traveling upward. A diffuser can also be put at the bottom of a lamp shade to keep the light at a higher level, or to hide the light source and thus prevent the unpleasant sight of the bulb when you are sitting next to or under the lamp.

A French *bouillotte* lamp (a tole or metalware-shaded lamp) can break the monotony of too many conventional lamp shades. These lamps offer several options. If yours is not actually old, you could paint the tole shade, say, an ivory with vertical stripes in black, green, or caramel, and then wax it to look old and worn. You could also paint the shade in a solid color and polish it with a yellow wax to achieve the patina of age. Terra-cotta, black, smoky blue, mushroom, red, dark green, or mottled white tole shades on silver or brass lamp bases look quite authentic. You can use bouillotte lamps in pairs, but more often you will see a single one on a desk for reading. I like to put real wax candles in the candle holder and use a double gooseneck mechanism that holds two bulbs in the middle, hidden nicely under the metal shade. This gives the choice of lighting the candle or reading by a stronger electric source. And by wiring the lamp this way, you avoid using flame-shaped bulbs in the candle holders.

There are times when it is necessary to expose the bulbs on a chandelier because shades are not the right solution. In such a case, I use tiny rounded, bullet-shaped bulbs—not easy to find, but they are available— or small, very thin frosted bulbs. The most unpleasant-looking bulbs imaginable are the big faux-flame-tipped ones. I cringe when I see them in hallways and vestibules; they are usually clear with a silly-looking loop at the top meant to resemble a flame. Not only have I never seen flames that look like that, but clear bulbs cast unattractive shadows on ceilings and walls; if they are on a chandelier hanging too low in a dining room, these shadows will be cast on the faces of the people around the table.

Years ago, when I did not know how to produce the quality of light I wanted, I would use a theatrical amber gel on lightbulbs to create a mellow glow at night. None of the bulbs encountered at that time gave the desired effect; the light was always too cold, casting a green or blue tinge into the room. Today there are so many kinds of bulbs available, but I still wish I could find a single bulb that is perfect for everything.

Creating the look of natural light with artificial lighting remains a challenge. A room may be marvelous in the daytime, but at night something unexpected can occur. If only it were possible to get the feeling of true candlelight with electric lighting. Candlelight makes everything golden, which is why the mood it creates is so romantic.

Lighting any kind of art must be done subtly. Spotlighting a painting with pin lights is especially unattractive, for it makes the art look like an image on a television set built into the wall. Paintings look best when the whole wall is softly washed in light. Certain bulbs will distort the

**Very little changes in my living
room, with the seasonal exception of slipcovers and flowers.**

colors of the picture, so it is important to choose a light that will truly
convey the hues the artist intended. Low-voltage halogen lighting,
which gives off a cool, clear, white light, is excellent for this task. Weldon lighting is particularly impressive. Its liabilities are that it is quite
expensive, that the transformer has to be built into the ceiling, and that
it is larger than the average recessed housing, but the trade-off is that it
reveals only dime-sized openings in the ceiling. Most wall washers are
much larger than Weldon lighting, but they are also effective.

We have much to learn in trying to emulate the wonders of natural
light in a lighting plan for art. At noon the strong rays of the sun cast
shadows in their wake, and often it is the shadows that give objects
dimension, definition, and texture. Lighting a piece of sculpture from
the side can define its shape even more than lighting it completely from
above. Each piece must be considered individually.

In my London flat, I have painted the walls a soft, amber-melon shade to counteract the usual bleakness of the foggy English weather—a glowing color in a gray climate. Londoners are often weather-weary and pray for a gay, sunny day, but to me the silvery, translucent light of a rainy day is pleasantly ethereal. It is an interesting change from the constant clear weather in the American West, and I do enjoy the chance to experience the wider range of emotions offered with the changing seasons.

Wherever we may be, there are times even during the day when natural light needs the assistance of artificial light. Though I am never completely satisfied with electric light during the day, every lighting plan should specify the lights to be used in the daytime: desk or reading lights, kitchen and bathroom lighting, and on somber, overcast days, some added ambient lighting. It is a challenge to balance and layer this light, to evenly disperse it throughout the room, rather than all in one area.

There are times when skylights can work wonders. They tend to bring the eye upward, adding not only light but additional height to an area. But again balance is important, and simply cutting open a skylight in a dark area can throw an entire room out of equilibrium. Too much light in one location and not enough in the rest of the space creates shadows and can throw off the harmony of the entire room. This situation presented itself when I was lighting the extremely dark entry of a house that was being remodeled. We installed a traditional museum-type skylight at the top of the stairs, but it gave so much light to one area that it had to be toned down with a filter.

Rooms that receive natural light from only one angle will have light at only certain times of day, and the remainder of the room will rest in shadow. While this may be fine in small areas, such as bathrooms, in larger areas it is a blessing to have more than one source of natural light. Mirrors are a way of introducing additional light into a room. Placed opposite a window, they can re-create the feeling of an additional window, and reintroduce the view. This can be a delightful option even in a small room. For example, I was able to make the joys of a bathtub in an alcove under a window even more rewarding by mirroring its other two sides, so that the experience of bathing included being surrounded by the garden outside. (See photo on page 193.)

In addition to increasing the size of windows or changing windows into French doors, you can add glass panels to existing doors to let the outdoor light in. This can be a solution for a dark entry, although privacy also must be considered. And, as mentioned before, whenever changing a window or adding a door, be scrupulous in considering the interior and exterior elevations of the house. Of course, many houses could have their integrity improved upon by the careful replanning and reproportioning of openings. An architecturally unattractive house can often be improved by the discerning eye of an architect or designer who may suggest alternatives to the existing windows and doors. While architectural imperfections can at times be successfully camouflaged by professional landscaping, nothing is a true substitute for proper, classic proportions. Consider that when one is inside, it does feel far nicer to have some light glowing outside, for looking out into complete blackness can be a bit spooky. Nonetheless, I like to use the minimum amount of artificial light possible. To turn into a private driveway and be bombarded by glowing pools of light everywhere, with every tree and path so lit up you could see a spider weaving its web, is not at all romantic. And *moonlighting,* as it is called, does not look anything like what happens when an area is actually lit by the moon.

At night, a garden should glow as if it were softly lit by the reflection of a sunset, not chilled by cold white or green lights. Illuminate your trees with very soft, pale light and try to make your light sources invisible. This is not always possible, but new lighting techniques are being discovered every day. Remember the cities and gardens that are truly magical for the way they are illuminated after dark. How wonderful the Palace of Versailles is at night, glowing and fiery! And Paris, the most beautiful city in the world in the daytime, is perhaps even more so at night, when the very best of its boulevards and buildings are aglow and the not-so-perfect buildings seem to be in hidden in shadow. To arrive in Paris after dark and to drive by the Arc de Triomphe, with its superb architecture and night lighting, always makes my heart stop.

On my first trip to Venice, we arrived at night in a small speedboat, which gave us a most spectacular introduction to that extraordinary city. It was so intoxicating that I had to rest my eyes every few minutes. Because of the way the city was lit I could see none of the decay, only the glory that is still Venice, wrapped in a golden glow. What makes

RIGHT) **For me, furniture must have personality as well as be beautiful. Finding this rare Italian table was a collector's dream. BELOW) Simple, comfortable upholstered seating is absolutely essential and gives other special pieces a wonderful backdrop.**

these magnificent places so special at night is the quality and the color of their lighting. I do wonder why I find the lighting of my simple garden so difficult.

One of the most rewarding aspects of contemporary architecture is the freedom with which light can be introduced into a space. If one chooses to draw from the past, buildings must honor period forms. Windows and door openings should follow the guidelines that were set by preceding generations, and these sometimes restrict and limit the amount of light that can be infused into a space. However, modern architecture is not restricted by historical forms and can be lit as the designer wishes. Windows need not conform to a particular style or shape; they can be newly created with each application. The architects of today forge their own paths, and while their art sometimes acknowledges precedents, it does not depend on them.

In both contemporary and traditional applications, the more numerous the sources of light, the less work must be rendered by each source. There will also be less of a contrast between the light and its surroundings. But I never advocate solving every lighting challenge by simply adding more sources. This approach has flaws as well, the primary one being that it creates too many openings and spots of light on the walls and ceilings.

Even candles can be overdone. In my living room, there are many places for candles—on the bookshelves, the tables, the stone mantels, even suspended from walls—and I once lit them all. The effect was vastly different from what I had expected. There were too many small, flickering points of light, and they made the room look agitated rather than restful. I have learned instead to keep candles close together in a few carefully planned groups, rather than dispersed throughout a room.

In designing with light, we work on many levels and scales. Lighting a small dressing room or bathroom can be as problematic as resolving the placement of windows for an entire house. Not only must one have focused light to apply makeup or to shave, but it is also important to be able to see yourself from head to toe in the proper light. On many lighting plans, the lighting in a bathroom is concentrated only on the area where the makeup is applied or the shaving takes place, which is usually over the sink. The rest of the room is often thrown into shadow.

In my flat in London the bathroom is tiny and entirely composed of bright white painted paneling, with insets of mirror throughout. When I first moved in, I did not pay much attention to the lighting on my face. But after spending three weeks in the city, with its foggy light and smoky silver skies, I came back to the bright California light to see that my eyebrows had almost grown together, and I had never even noticed! I immediately set out to improve the light around my small vanity in London. I installed lights that bounce off the high-gloss surface of the bathroom walls and are multiplied by all the mirrors. The lighting above the sink is recessed right over the mirror and does not shine down on my face but rather allows the light to fall in front of me.

Whatever its size, make an effort not to have your bathroom look like a waterproofed site in which to perform minor surgeries. Instead, it should feel like an extension of the adjoining room. Never think of a bathroom as anything other than an entire room, one that must be as charming as any room in the house. Its decorative elements just happen to be big, soft towels and perhaps a wonderful woven rug, lovely bottles of scent, books, windows with filmy curtains, flowers, and either simple, crisp fabrics or colorful, printed ones. In any bathroom, consider what your eyes fall upon when you sit in your steamy, scented tub. If you are fortunate, it will be a window with a garden view.

Planning new construction provides the perfect opportunity to turn your attention not only to the lighting but to the layout of the space. If possible, it would be far more pleasant not to walk into a bath or powder room and be directly facing the commode. The ideal solution is to have it in its own tiny enclosure. If the area is too small to accommodate a separate space—and this is true of most baths—then it should be situated behind the door, hidden until you close the door behind you. This is an easy and excellent solution, yet one that is almost always overlooked.

Everyone has their own preferences when it comes to lighting a makeup table or your basin. You may find that an even, theatrical, straight-on *key* light is your favorite way to light your face. If you manage to look fairly attractive with the hideous overhead lighting so often

A Japanese wood-and-ivory cage stands on a shelf. Beneath is a collection of Roman glass on a narrow and unusually long Ming stand. A Richard Serra painting sits on an early Spanish table.

found in bathrooms or dressing areas, then you know you will actually look fabulous in the soft lights of the party you are attending—but only if the light strikes the middle of your face and not under the chin. On the other hand, key light, where the whole face is evenly lit, may lead you to wish to stay home, because you will never look as glamorous anywhere else.

Great hostesses pay very strict attention to lighting, as I was reminded when two European friends came to stay and help me plan a dinner party. I will not mention their names here, for to do so would make their future guests aware of the kind of attention they pay to detail and would dampen the pleasure of being entertained in an atmosphere that seems spontaneous, although it has been brilliantly planned to the smallest degree.

There was to be an important guest at my dinner party who held a special fascination for one of my visiting friends. I can remember her exact words to me the evening before the dinner: "Rose, we must see how you are planning to seat this dinner. Could you possibly set out the candles that are to be on the table?"

I was planning to serve a Chinese dinner, and the table would have to hold many dishes. This being so, I explained that I would have candles only on the perimeter of the room and in the iron chandelier that hangs over the table.

"Oh, no," she cried, "that will never do. There must be candlelight at the table." Obediently, I lit the candles and dimmed the lights that washed the sideboard and the tapestry on the wall. Off to her room went my friend; she soon returned wearing a deep red sweater. (I had not realized that this was to be a dress rehearsal!) At the table, she positioned herself briefly in the different seats so that we could determine where the light hit her in the kindest, most rewarding way. We could observe how the reflections bouncing back from the window affected the room: one side of the table was nicely lit, but the other side was not nearly as flattering.

Now, where to place the honored guest, and next to whom should he be seated? Should he be across or down the table from my friend? It was decided that it was far more provocative to have her across the table so that they could gaze at each other from afar. We also decided that we were not mad about the deep red sweater, so she changed to a white satin shirt, which reflected the candlelight beautifully.

Anticipation is sometimes far more fun than any actual event. The intimacy and joy of playing dress-up games with my two dear friends that evening turned out to be considerably more stimulating than entertaining the not-so-very-enthralling-after-all Mr. Wonderful at dinner the following evening!

Patterns and Textures

Designing with fabric has always been an exacting and time-consuming process for me. I had my first experience with this when I was a very young bride-to-be. I assembled twenty different white fabrics from which to choose my wedding dress. I lived with them for what seemed like an eternity before I could make a decision—touching, and crushing, and playing with the materials for days before finally settling on a paper silk taffeta. This was only a portent of what was to come. Another clue to my peculiarly discriminating nature emerged when I was selecting fabrics for the few pieces of furniture in my first house; I assembled not twenty but perhaps hundreds of samples from which to choose. I was unable to settle for something that did not seem exactly right. I visited and revisited Scalamandre, a well-established fabric house, until I became a familiar figure. Though I did not realize it at the time, this was the first step toward my future career. Now, years later, after decades of training and experience, and even after designing fabrics for Scalamandre and for Melrose House, selection has not become any easier for me. I still spend hours studying and handling a fabric. There are times when I drive around for days with a particular material on the dashboard of my car before I can decide whether to use it.

A successful fabric-filled room that delights the eye rarely happens by itself. Magic needs a magician. The magician spends hours practicing pulling pigeons out of a hat, yet when he presents them to his audience, the performance looks as easy as pie. The same is true with decorating. Putting together the right fabrics to create a marvelous room requires enormous thought, yet with all that expended energy, the finished space must feel and look as natural, relaxed, and carefree as possible. Sometimes you may want to introduce an unexpected twist into a room—a pillow of a completely different color, or a chair painted in a surprisingly unrelated shade. These quirky additions divert the eye from any propensity for perfection. Again, perfection can be perfectly boring.

Working with fabric and light must go hand in hand. Many rooms need some type of fabric treatment on the windows to soften and filter the light that enters them, and to give them a completed feel. Other rooms need help with scale and proportions. Valances can be used to reproportion a window that needs heightening, whereas shutters and side panels can visually add width. However, deep cornices and heavy curtains will generally look ponderous except in period rooms where they are welcome. Elaborate curtain treatments are especially unappealing on sliding modern doors, or on any long expanse of windows. A long wall completely covered with heavy fabric curtains looks not unlike a movie theater. Similarly, lavish billows and festoons are meant as much to keep out the cold as to dress a room, so they are often oppressive and unsuitable in warm or tropical climates. I am often asked why I cringe when students continually refer to "drapes." To this I quote Nancy Mitford's *Noblesse Oblige,* "Drapes—this word is an inexcusable vulgarism. Curtains are hung at a window."

Today, there are lighter, more contemporary approaches to covering a window. There are many interesting types of shades, blinds, and shutters available today. In contemporary rooms, venetian blinds are a simple, yet strong solution. When designing any room, whether contemporary or traditional, allow light and air to enter freely to keep it cool and comfortable by day and pleasantly romantic and glowing in the evening.

Other than in the Early American context of a low-ceilinged room, using a deep valance and heavy curtains can have a comical effect. When choosing your window treatments, keep in mind that festooned curtains, swags, and their counterparts will look as out of place in most low-ceilinged rooms as a short person in a ballooning evening dress. Today I like to dress windows very simply. If a valance is called for, consider using a tailored, soft one with a center pleat and corner pleats. A thin vertical stripe can help elongate the window or doors. Another way to create the illusion of height is to position the valance a distance above the top of the window. Then place a bamboo or fabric shade directly under it to cover the top of the window frame and hide the fact that the window does not actually meet the valance. But look at all the openings in the room before you do this: will the taller window now make the door openings look poorly proportioned? It is best not to use tiebacks when you want to create the illusion of height. Instead, let the curtains hang straight and naturally. If some type of pulling back is required, a theatrical draw can be very effective. This is made by loosely threading a piece of cord through rings sewn on the back of the curtain and softly drawing it up in a light gather.

Designing a guest room, even if it is tiny, is the perfect opportunity to

PRECEDING PAGE) **An octagonal guest bath–sitting room
where the shower, closets,
and bathroom accessories
are housed behind paneled
doors.** RIGHT) **A Queen Anne
cabinet in a guest bedroom
once belonged to the Duke
and Duchess of Windsor.**

indulge a love for fabric. A profusion of designs in a small room softens
into perimeters and makes the space feel larger than it actually is. You
can see this effect in miniature if you take a small box and cover it
entirely in a printed paper—it will be transformed into something quite
seamless and special.

Have you noticed that when you're using printed fabric in any room,
the more of it you use, the better it looks? In my very first bedroom, I
covered the bed and hung the windows in a red-and-white toile de
Jouy linen. It was not that interesting, and after a while I decided to
cover the walls and all the furniture in the same fabric. This transformed
the room immediately and made it quite cozy and intimate.

Even the most monochromatic color scheme yearns for, at the very
least, a brief encounter with some interesting pattern. Maybe a wonderful rug is all the room needs, or perhaps the pattern will come in the
form of a drawing, a painting, or a chair or pillow covered in a delicate

print. In the grand style of traditional European homes, an eighteenth-century Beauvais tapestry, a Gobelin tapestry, or some English needlepoint will contribute undeniable richness of texture. They have the handwoven intricacy and dignity of pattern that most new fabrics have not had the time to acquire.

Old textiles and tapestries can often offer the magic needed to soften the pristine quality of a freshly decorated room. New tapestries, however, can bring a false note into a room. A pillow made out of a beautiful, worn, old fragment of velvet has far more appeal than a machine-woven new tapestry. (As yet, I have never seen an exceptional reproduction of an old tapestry.)

In designing interiors, the selection of fabrics can be one of the most creative tasks imaginable. In the early stages of a project, you may have some preconceived ideas about the fabrics and color schemes you plan to use. But before any defining decisions are made, visit a few textile houses; you may discover a new color or pattern that inspires you. When this happens, it is sometimes as revitalizing as it is problematic, especially if the entire plan is already in place in your mind's eye. The lesson here is not to make any definite commitments until you have seen everything possible.

When choosing a fabric, decide upon one that resonates with the effect and mood you wish to create. You should approach prints and solids differently. With a print, first determine how it will be used. Perhaps you envision it for the upholstery. Remember that even when backed, lightweight materials are not as durable on frequently used furniture as heavier fabrics. (But this has rarely deterred me from using them!) The alternative to upholstering furniture is to use slipcovers. Slipcovering allows you to grow tired of a fabric and change it from time to time. Besides giving a lovely unstructured look to a room, slip-covers offer the additional luxury of being easily refreshed.

When covering large soft seating such as a sofa or armchair, look for a solid material that will upholster well. Fabric has its foibles. If it could be chosen for its beauty alone, decisions would be simpler. But not all that is beautiful is malleable, so never set your heart on a fabric without manipulating it first. Take it in hand, bend it, and fold it to test its texture and resilience. Wooden-framed chairs and benches do not usually present as much of a problem; since they are tightly upholstered, their fabric does not need to give as much. Fully upholstered pieces, on the other hand, do require consideration. Is the material you are thinking about using pliable? Will it melt into the form of the sofa? Will it make a proper flat seam?

Small rooms can be wonderfully intimate. In these rooms, small patterns look delightful, perhaps joined by an even smaller-scale design. If you are working with a multicolored floral chintz fabric, you may want to introduce a solid texture, or perhaps a stripe, plaid, or check fabric somewhere in the room. The challenge is to keep the combination of all these different materials from actually looking too contrived.

Textures in textiles can give needed variation to a room. A monochromatic palette without different textures will result in a bland, monotonous room. Textural interest can be introduced in numerous ways—in finishes, curtains, wall hangings, tapestries, antique cloths, and carpets. There might be, for example, some large pieces, such as sofas and club chairs, covered in a velvet rib, with another piece or two in a soft leather; the carpet could be in straw, with chintz curtains, cashmere throws, a needlepoint bench, and satin or taffeta pillows placed on a sofa or chair.

I have learned an amazing amount from the upholstered furniture

A corner of a guest bedroom.
Because the walls are paneled,
I have used lots of dark
lacquer in the room.

pieces made in our workrooms. Unusual fabrics arrive daily from different designers, and this has shown me what can be expected from each material. On my own pieces I query, is the quality thin enough to make the delicate flat welt that I prefer? Or will I need to find a small, simple cord welt of a different material or a woven cord to work with it? Even if the fabric would make a nice clean single welt, would using a banding of a different material, maybe even a contrasting one, enhance the piece as a whole? If you use a heavy, solid-colored upholstery fabric, consider finding a very soft piece of leather or suede and making the trim out of that. Leather is sometimes too heavy-handed, but on a solid, masculine fabric and piece it could be just the added texture that is needed.

It is important to respect the period of a piece of furniture, which includes putting the right covering on it. I require my design students to research period fabrics and study how they pertain to the furniture of their time. Once, an astute class member asked me when it was acceptable to use a textile not of the period on an antique chair, as I had just told them that it is easy to spot a novice by the fabric they use on such pieces. To put a stripe on a Louis XV fauteuil would be the disturbing choice, as would be a cut-velvet flame stitch. To put a William Morris design on a Queen Anne chair of any merit would also not be in keeping with the period of the piece, nor would a patterned chintz work on a Russian settee. We could go on for hours like this, but the question my student had in mind was rather how he could break the rules successfully without disrespecting the integrity of the piece. My answer was that it is not necessary to use a period fabric as long as you choose a covering that has no conflicting or defining date of origin. Thankfully, there are many more fabrics that do not have an identifiable period than there are those that do. I feel that it is imperative that all students of design learn the rules of their craft before they decide whether or not to break them. An educated decision is far better than an uninformed one.

There is a shop in Paris that deals only in remnants of period fabrics. The pieces are all meticulously stacked in piles and encased in cabinets behind glass doors. Unless you know exactly what you are looking for —what material and from which period—you will be shown very little or perhaps nothing at all. The first time I went there, I had no specific idea what I was looking for; I simply wished to be inspired by heaps of antique material.

I was very interested to see what treasures were in those tall wood and glass cabinets, so I asked for a Louis XVI stripe—a safe choice because I adore stripes, and at least it meant I would be shown something. Unfortunately, this tactic did not produce results, and I was asked to be more specific. Did I want a velvet stripe, a silk, a taffeta, or cotton?

Would it be possible to see everything, all the Louis XVI stripes, I asked. Madame the shopkeeper still refrained from showing me anything, as I was apparently not saying whatever it was she wanted to hear. When I become particularly tired, lazy, frustrated, or flustered, my ability to communicate in French diminishes considerably—this was beginning to manifest itself. After a bit more dialogue, Madame finally showed me the Louis XVI stripes she had, which, by the way, consisted of six small remnants of some very grand period pieces. After complimenting their quality and saying a few things that would show I was a seriously interested designer, I asked to see her Directoire and Empire stripes and her small Empire-period prints. Again, she opened her cabinet and unrolled a few fabrics. There was one particularly lovely remnant that I told her I was interested in having, and she set it aside. Her stern manner seemed to soften, and we began a conversation of sorts, although not a very cozy one; at least she seemed satisfied that I was not wasting her time.

The fabrics were all gems, each carefully rolled and tied with a ribbon in a simple and exquisitely ordered way. Just seeing the manner in which they were stored was reward enough for being there. It took what seemed to be hours of wooing and cajoling to go through some of her collection, one piece at a time; it was like playing a game of strip poker with an unwilling partner. I finally left, blissfully happy, with a wonderful satin stripe of aqua and white, water-stained and yellowing. I have never paid such a high price for any fabric, in terms of both time and money. Since that trip, years ago, I have become a welcomed client in the shop and have often found very special fabrics, but none that I like as well as my first purchase.

Collecting old fabrics is a passion of mine, although my usual haunts are far less intimidating than the shop in Paris. I look for fabrics everywhere, and have done so for years, long before I ever had thoughts of designing or manufacturing them myself. What I have learned from my collections is that using old and new fabrics in the same context is a challenge; it is not always easy to integrate them. The old can put the new fabric to shame because it is mellow and worn. Conversely, an old fabric can lose its vitality when it is mixed with the new, and may even appear dingy. I sometimes use old fragments of fabric in my shop to cover new pieces of furniture. An old material can add a special patina to a new piece of furniture, but it has to be just the right fabric, since a fabric that is too worn may sadly diminish the freshness of the whole.

Consider paneling and *boiserie* as wall coverings, along with wallpaper and material. Wood paneling is a wonderful addition to a room. Putting

Geometric fabrics and floral prints, pattern on pattern, are delightful in combination with the Polonaise carpet in a guest bedroom.

closets behind hidden panels in dressing areas will also afford more living space. In my bedroom closet, behind panels I have three tiers of clothing that reach almost all the way to the top of my fourteen-foot ceiling. This may sound awkward, but I rotate my clothes with the seasons; before summer, I put all my winter clothes on the top row, and in September, they are reversed. I rarely design walk-in closets: not only do they take up too much space but they display clothes in a way that always seems disorderly. I would rather see one group of clothing at a time behind doors. If everything is separated—suits, dresses, skirts, slacks, and so on—it is neater and less confusing. When I moved into my house, I had special hangers covered in the same fabric I used in my drawers and in the lining of the canopy of my bed. I purposely have never ordered more. Whenever I go on a shopping spree, I know that I must dispose of as many things in my closet as I have just bought. I do the same thing with shoes: two pairs in, two pairs out. I prefer this

A dining room I designed in
Australia offers a whimsical
interpretation of what one
might expect to find in the
Brighton Pavilion. The woodwork was created from actual
bamboo. In the same room are
a pair of seventeenth-century
screens and tole trees from
the Regency period.

arrangement; it is an excellent system for living within the limits of my closet space.

When I was building the house, I had just recently finished constructing one where we had designed a spacious dressing room and closet for the lady of the house. We had been given explicit instructions as to what she wanted, and she had specified room for her sixty long gowns. Months later, I momentarily forgot myself when I was designing the closet space for my own house. I kept reiterating that I needed lots of hanging space for my long gowns. After a while, my contractor looked at me with a quizzical expression in his eyes and asked, "Just how many gowns do you have?" I thought for a minute and then answered in a tiny voice, "One." A perfect example of getting carried away by one's own inflated sense of importance!

Fabric and paper can aid in hiding a multitude of problems and structural deficiencies. But when covering a wall with fabric, consider using very little padding behind it, so that you do not feel you are in a cushioned box. Padding is best in areas that are not used on a daily basis, such as guest rooms, guest powder rooms, and occasionally family bedrooms. Indeed, if it were not for the fact that I like the seams to be sewn, I would always have fabric backed with paper and hung as wallpaper. I like to trim solid fabrics with a flat welt of the same fabric or a small cord of either the same or a contrasting color.

With the exception of old Chinese papers, many of us tend to lose patience with wallpaper and want to change it after a few years. The same can be true with wall-to-wall carpet. I like to feel a cool, clean bare floor under my feet or, alternatively, an area rug. Yet an interesting wall-to-wall woven carpet can do wonders to pull a room together and create an ordered effect. In summer, expanses of woolen carpeting can

In this tiny jewel box of a bedroom in London, the overscaled furniture and patterned taffeta curtains contribute to making it the most intimate and cozy room imaginable.

feel and look heavy. There are times when upholstered walls can feel the same, especially if the fabric is heavy. Try using lightweight fabrics when covering walls; otherwise, you may be tempted to pull it off and let the walls breathe. To enjoy a plain surface, to feel comfortable with the change of seasons, I would think that the walls would want some air. Can you imagine wearing the same outfit year in and year out?

Bedrooms and guest rooms are favorite places for using printed fabrics. Bedrooms usually contain no overpowering pieces of sculpture or large paintings, so pattern is not an intrusion. Bedrooms also have standard pieces of furniture in them: a bed, a nightstand or two, a few comfortable chairs, and, if there is space, a small writing table and a cabinet.

These are the most introverted, private rooms in the house. In the decorative sense they are the one place where anything is acceptable. The ultimate question for any bedroom or guest bedroom is: Would you be happy holed up in this room for a week with another person? Bedrooms simply must be comfortable. A bedroom will inevitably be more intimate, introverted, and reflective of its occupant's personality than any of the other areas of the household. It is here that one places personal photos and other memento pieces to create a cozy atmosphere. A bedroom can be crowded, warm, and enveloping, or spare, fresh, light-filled, and modern. One thing is completely evident, however: without the essence of its inhabitants, a bedroom is no more or less than a hotel room.

For centuries, the bed was the most luxurious item in the house, and more fabric was lavished on it than on any other piece of furniture. The French would frame their beds in garlands of fanciful fabrics, creating stages for sleeping and lounging. The *lit de repos* was for daytime dalliances, and there are also the *duchesse en bateau* and the *duchesse brisée*: one is a chaise enclosed at the bottom like a small boat, and the other is the same chaise cut in half—a wood-framed chair and ottoman, literally "a broken duchess." In the nineteenth century, during the Directoire and Empire periods, campaign beds became fashionable. These could be simple or thoroughly decorated with masculine motifs; they would be folded and taken into battle tents.

The English designed beds one could hide in for a week and not be found. They were little rooms in themselves. Made of oak and walnut, the early beds were heavily carved and covered in tapestries and rich velvet brocades, offering sanctuaries of warmth during the cold English winters. As time passed, these beds lost their four-sided walls and became less of a warm little room and more of an open stage. Enter the four-poster, today the most favored of beds. Very few of us can resist having at least one four-poster in our lives. It is whimsical, fanciful, and utterly luxurious to sleep in a fabric-swathed bed. Even the most understated and contemporary house will often harbor a dreamy, romantic four-poster.

Designing a bedroom is like entertaining on Thanksgiving—you do not have to be unusually inventive with the menu because much of it is prescribed by tradition and practical necessities. But it always helps to be a bit creative with the ingredients. And remember that patterned fabrics and overscaled furniture always look wonderful in small spaces. Aside from the requisite bed, put in a bedroom exactly what you need to be comfortable: a writing table, a chair, a television, a night table, and a dressing table. A chaise longue is a delightful luxury, but not always possible. Night tables need to have a place for plenty of reading material, good lighting, and a telephone. The fabric we use on our bedroom windows should be carefully considered, since they give us our first glimpse of the morning, forming our first impressions of the day.

Guest rooms should adhere to the same standards. To be sure it is well planned, spend a weekend in your guest room. Constantly refurbish it

A house should be timeless;
this room in my London
flat has remained the same
for twenty years. Only a very
few refurbishing changes
ever take place.

and never neglect the details, the same items that make your own bed-room comfortable—fresh flowers and fruit, updated reading, a clock, stationery, stamps, and so forth. The guest bath should have aspirin, lux-urious toweling, robes, deliciously fragrant soap, bath oils, perfumes, and a wide variety of sundries.

There are times the master bedroom is *not* the most private room in the house. If you have a young family, you may find that your bed becomes a gathering place. Those weekend mornings with my youngest son, Jon, snuggled under my covers are memories I still hold close in my heart. And so designing a bedroom also requires attention to the differ-ent stages of its inhabitants' lives. For a young family, the room will be a delicious mix of comfort and coziness, with fabrics that are machine-washable and lots of places for children to sit, perhaps to watch a movie, do a puzzle, or color a picture. When you are a parent, wherever you are is where your children want to be; when they grow up a bit, the truth

A marvelous pair of
eighteenth-century dark
mahogany cabinets frame
a doorway in this pale
pine-paneled living room.

may be just the opposite, and then perhaps it will be time to indulge in a more romantic bedroom.

Ana and Joef (my second, inherited family), are constantly in our bedroom when they are home from college, just as they were when they were younger. They watch a late-night movie there, talk on the phone, read, or just spend time with us. The intimacy of sharing this space with them is a pleasure that surpasses any need for privacy.

Whatever else it is, the bedroom is a place to wake up to the world in peace. In the early morning, lying in the cocoon of your bed, you can meditate on the future of your day, your week, your life. Through the window you can see if it is sunny, rainy, or snowing; you cannot change the weather, but you can change how you choose to react to it, and that will absolutely be influenced by how comfortable you are in your surroundings.

As a rule, my favorite rooms fall into two categories: those that have enormous presence, great scale, and high ceilings, and rooms that are quite small with interesting proportions. My bedroom in London is one of those lovely little rooms, so irresistible that one might hope to have the flu just to spend a week in bed there, all cozy and cocooned. The curtains are blue-and-white taffeta, with a medium-scaled flower print in different shades of blue. They have been in place for almost twenty years and are fraying a bit now at the edges. On the wooden floor lies a blue-and-antique-white linen Agra carpet with an allover pattern. A chair and ottoman, a bed, and a prie-dieu are the entire extent of the furniture. While the chair and ottoman are of normal size, they are larger than you might expect in such a small room. I could have used smaller pieces, but then the room would not look, or be, as comfortable as it is (see page 183).

To me, the fantasy of living in a nun's cell is pure heaven. I imagine a bed covered in a creamy, heavy hemp fabric in a tiny room that has rough, whitewashed plaster walls, a small Gothic window, a stone sink; outside a bird sings. Peace prevails. But, where would I put the television, the stacks of books, the clothes and shoes, the telephone, the reading lamp, and the chaise longue? It seems I would be none too good at being a nun.

I do not limit my love of small rooms to bedrooms. I am always attracted by small rooms in large houses. At Versailles, the rooms I covet are the tiny antechambers. In many houses, you will notice that people are drawn to the smallest sitting room. We all love to crowd into close spaces for hours, perhaps to read, listen to music, or watch a film. If the room is comfortable to sit in, then drawing people out of it requires enormous effort, a bit like trying to get sardines out of a tin can. I was at a dinner recently where the hostess was doing her best to tempt the guests out of the tiny library and into the more spacious and newly designed drawing room by offering drinks in the larger room. No one would budge; they would take the bait but then immediately jump back into the small pond of the cozy little room.

Nearly every favorite small room has a piece of furniture that is a bit overscaled. There is one charming country room in England that I will never forget. I was in it only once, for grog early on a Christmas Day. The room was packed with people. The ceilings were back-bendingly low in areas and had dark wooden beams in odd places. Bunches of mistletoe were tied with red ribbon and hung from the doorways; the windows were narrow and had wonderful old uneven panes of glass in them; the walls were white and chalky, and the few pieces of furniture were large and spare. The room felt like it had been mellowed by pleasure and time. The sagging but comfortable sofa had a portly mastiff

Windows frame the bathtub in
this guest bathroom: to feel as
if you are bathing in a garden
is pure bliss.

lounging on it. A stone fireplace in the corner of the room was lit and doing its best to heat the room, although we were grateful for our hot toddies, which were strong enough to warm the hands and heart.

The proportions of the room were perfect, with leaded windows on two walls. The focal point was a superb wooden stable door that was well waxed and strapped in early ironwork. Yes, it was a stable door, and it opened in the middle, just as stable doors do. The house was in the village of Sonning and had once belonged to Dick Turpin, the infamous highwayman. When he was working at his regular profession of highway robbery, he often was called upon to make a quick getaway. His horse could not be any nearer, since the stable door opened right into Turpin's living room. All he had to do was pull on his pants, fling open the door, jump on his horse, and ride off in the nick of time!

At Your Feet

PRECEDING PAGE) **A beautiful Queen Anne tea table stands in front of an antique settee still covered in its original leather. The Kashgar carpet is interwoven with combination silver and burnished metal threads.** RIGHT) **A Georgian settee has been placed on an Amritsar carpet.**

In 1990, I finished work on a house in Australia that was a complete departure from any house I had ever designed. The structure had just been completed when I was introduced to the clients. It was a grand house, in both size and design. My clients loved life, color, and the prospect of continuous entertaining. I was asked to create a formal dining room, which needed to seat no fewer than twenty-four at any meal and, a good deal of the time, as many as sixty. The clients wanted a dining room that would be a change from what they were used to, so I suggested a room that took its inspiration from the Brighton Pavilion, built in the early nineteenth century for the Prince Regent after designs by John Nash and William Chambers. They were delighted when I proposed a whimsical interpretation of that style.

We found a Chinese cabinetmaker who could work with real bamboo, imported from China in many different circumferences. On page 180 is the only photograph ever taken of the completed room. From

this angle and distance, it is difficult to appreciate the beauty of the bamboo, but what made the room so charming was the variety of sizes and colors of the wood. It would not have been nearly as effective had it been attempted with faux bamboo. It took ages to create the paneling, as the Chinese cabinetmaker was committed to very definite and very traditional methods of installation. Every piece of bamboo had to face a certain direction so as to emit a positive energy. We added a pair of wonderful seventeenth-century Chinese screens on the walls. Designed especially for the room, the fabric for the curtains was a crisp, flat, cream silk taffeta with bright blue-green and apricot satin stripes; they hung simply from behind the cornices. The chairs were covered in a heavy, ribbed silk apricot fabric. The final effect was quite charming.

The challenge of Chinese cabinetmaking would be a fairly arcane area of woodworking for any decorator. A far more mundane use of wood would seem to be flooring. But simple it is not. For years, I struggled with every flooring dilemma that could possibly face a designer. When I first left design school I had no idea how to work with floor finishers. Today, I can hardly believe that I was so poorly equipped to handle this important job. I was able to distinguish between the different periods of wood flooring—which were used in the seventeenth century, which were used in the eighteenth century, and the patterns of the different parquets—yet I was completely at a loss as to how to instruct a floor polisher to finish a floor.

Years later, when I began to design and manufacture furniture, my experience with wood and finishing was an enormous asset. And my work with antiques taught me a tremendous amount about woods; but even today, with more than twenty-five years of experience, I still have to cajole a new floor finisher into working with wood my way.

When considering choices for their wood floors, many people simply select red or white oak, yet there are a great number of other interesting possibilities. If the house is quite modern, you may want a wood that will bleach to a very light shade, perhaps ash, maple, or any number of woods that have a clean, simple, figured grain. Unlike oak's, the grain of these woods is pleasingly linear, but you will always need to check the grain carefully before using it in cabinetry or flooring.

Eighteenth-century European oak-plank or parquet floors are difficult to re-create. Old English and French oak is so different from the oak available today that there is hardly any similarity between the two. (Unless floorboards are authentically old, I would never consider the use of pegs.) Old pine can also be beautiful, but new pine is not easy to work with; I use it on floors that I plan to paint over. Similarly, new oak has a very open, porous grain and will soak up paint or stain, leaving dark, large unattractive grain patterns. It must be bleached to even out the color, unless, of course, you want the wood to be an exceptionally dark shade overall. Surprisingly, red oak is easier to bleach than white oak. The few truly successful oak floors are either very dark, bleached, or bleached and wire-brushed.

Think of using walnut on your floors. Walnut can be bleached until it is quite light, and then stained almost any medium shade. Its cost should be equal to that of oak, and the grain is superb. Because few people use walnut on floors today, a floor man may balk at the very suggestion. Remember, flooring companies do not like bleaching, and this wood may have to be bleached several times to get the kind of light, clear finish that is so lovely. I have heard many reasons given for not bleaching any kind of wood. Take no notice of such warnings: it is fine to bleach solid woods. We do it every day in our workshops. But even after years of experience working with wood, I always have samples made first and work with the color until I am completely satisfied.

LEFT) One of a pair of Regency chairs on an Empire marquetry floor. BELOW) A lovely old bamboo mat covering a portion of the nineteenth-century marquetry floor has a pleasantly quirky and softening effect in this otherwise serious entry hall.

When presented with the opportunity to lay new floorboards, design each room separately but always keep the whole in mind. I will often use the same size boards throughout a house, usually five-inch to ten-inch, or else random boards of several sizes. I define each room with its own border. Sometimes I will border the room and then let that border continue into the center, so that there will be a meeting of four triangles in the middle of the room.

In the photo on page 169, the octagonal bath–dressing room was created out of several small, adjoining dressing rooms and closets. I allowed the new shape of the room to dictate the way the floorboards lay. In the redesigned room, the seating, tub, and sink are all within the octagon, and the remaining bath utilities, shower, and closets are behind closed doors outside the octagon.

In remodeling an old house, you may be fortunate enough to lift up a carpet and find wide-plank wood subflooring. If the old floor is of good quality, coating it with paint is a bit hard to justify. However, if the planks are narrow subflooring, groove them to give the effect of wider planks, then sand and paint them. I would consider regrooving a floor only when it is to be painted.

Try using color on an old floor of inferior wood—black with small amounts of natural wood showing, or very dark green, white, or cream. One of the glorious characteristics of Early American decorative arts is the frequent use of colorful painted floors. Years ago, I evoked this look by stenciling an entry floor in dark caramel and ivory squares. I used many layers of paint and then varnished the top, which caused the ivory to turn a mellow shade. The effect was stunning.

A well-waxed wood floor is something to take pride in. Yet the introduction of a fine rug—perhaps an early Aubusson or Bessarabian—can transform the mood of an entire house. I am often torn between my passion for bare wood floors and my appreciation for fine carpets. It has, however, been my experience that a good rug is hard to find. With this fact always in mind, make allowances in your preliminary floor plan for several sizes of rugs: perhaps one under the main seating area, a smaller carpet under the coffee table, or even one that covers a good portion of the room. Planning for a variety of possible floor coverings gives you flexibility, but the carpet you eventually choose will often not be the size you drew onto your plan at the beginning. For your living room, do try to find a truly marvelous carpet. Be open to the unexpected treasure. Sometimes if a rug is a bit off in just the right way, it will add a refreshing element. This cannot be planned; when it happens, the rug offers the quirky twist that makes an entire room come alive.

Such delightful serendipity can also come from finding an unusual table or chair, an uncommon accessory, or even an unorthodox placement for a piece of furniture. I once completed a bedroom and yet, although I was pleased with the results, could not pronounce it finished. I looked through my stash of treasures, my odds and ends that have not as yet found a home, and came up with a beautiful piece of embroidered silk that had once been part of a priest's robe. I had taken it on consignment from a shop to try it in a different room, and its color and personality had nothing to do with what I was trying to accomplish in this bedroom. But when I placed it in the center of the bedspread, the room took on a new and far more interesting personality (see page 54). You can never second-guess how the magic will reveal itself.

The quest for the perfect old or antique carpet can be a time-consuming project, but it is well worth the effort. Once you have an idea of the size you would be interested in, then you can begin your search. Floor plan in hand, start by visiting merchants who deal in fine carpets. Do this even before you have a color scheme in mind, before any wall is painted or any window treated. Do not leave any possible rug unexamined. Even for a professional, it can be agonizingly boring to sit for hours in a stuffy room full of heavy rolls of rugs and have one carpet after another hurled at your feet. I have often done this for weeks at a time, traveling from one shop to the next, drinking endless cups of chewy coffee, in search of what I needed, and I have, more than once, come up empty-handed. By now, I have learned to read the backs of rug rolls and can pretty much eliminate the unattractive or unsuitable ones before they are unleashed. I can tell from the back side if the weave is too woolly and thick, if the pattern is unpleasantly vivid, or if the rug is entirely out of my color range. This can be tricky; since the vegetable dyes may have faded only on the face of the rug, the back side is usually much richer in color. If the dealer highly recommends a rug, I always look at it anyway.

When you find a carpet that you adore, you will be in the best of all possible positions. I say *adore* because there should be no compromise. A carpet is, in effect, a painting on the floor, and just as you would never hang an unattractive piece of art on the wall, never lay one on the floor. It is a blessing to find a fantastic rug and have the pattern and pace of the room set. With the right carpet, the upholstery, fabrics, wall colors, and curtain materials fall a little more easily into place.

Of course, you may not have the luxury of postponing work until the right rug comes along. Continue working without it, keeping in mind that you will either find the perfect rug or go another route. Because there is a definite chance that you may not find this special piece in time to meet your schedule, you must have an alternative plan in place.

Let us imagine that you are still looking for just the right piece, but

In the sitting area of a master bedroom, a seventeenth-century wall hanging can be used as a carpet because the foot traffic is light.

meanwhile you decide to move ahead with your plans. The first step in designing the room will then be to select a neutral background. By neutral, I mean you should create a room that dictates no definite color theme. Then you may select different fabrics that contain the same tone as your background and use them to cover your large, soft pieces of furniture. These fabrics, leathers, and coverings should be able to express themselves unaggressively and eventually can accommodate a wonderful pattern on the floor.

Since this type of room has no distracting colors or patterns to captivate the eye, its furnishings must be very carefully considered. The very quality of colorlessness dissolves space and positions your furniture, objects, and architecture in the forefront. The advantage of a monochromatic room is that many of the furnishings and accessories can be found or made early on, ready to complement the carpet they are waiting for. With this kind of palette, you will be able to adapt any carpet into the room at any time, up to and including the very last minute.

Carpets have extremely intrusive personalities, and so they represent a commitment you need to be absolutely sure about. You can move furniture about if it is necessary, and you can even discard certain pieces and acquire new ones, but good carpets are costly and do not lend themselves to that kind of flexibility.

Although your floor plan will always tell you whether a rug you are considering is the right size, it is useful to see it in its proposed setting, surrounded by the character and light of the room in which it will eventually be placed. Try to take carpets on consignment, even if they must be shipped from some distance. They can be rolled out, and if they are not just right, they can easily be rerolled, wrapped in their original packaging, and returned anywhere in the world within a day or so. Even if you feel absolutely certain that the carpet will be

ABOVE) These unusual
seventeenth-century Dutch
candleholders have an
eccentric charm. RIGHT) A
seventeenth-century Chinese
watercolor hangs on a pantry
wall next to a Welsh dugout
chair and antique porcelain
cabbage terrines. The floors
are simple bleached walnut.

the most perfect addition possible, you should still make every effort not to seal the bargain until you can actually see it in place.

Let us say you have finally found the piece you have been searching for. The dealer is happy, and so is the most difficult person to please: you. Now it is time to connect the carpet to its setting. Perhaps all you need to do to make the ultimate connection between rug and room is to add a piece of porcelain, or a few accessory pillows, or a bit of antique textile placed on the back of a chair or a sofa. If you are not convinced that the rug is integrated into the room, you may decide to cover a chair or a bench in a complementary fabric.

This type of integration is important at many levels of the design process. For example, a house that has just been built needs to anchor itself to its environment. Eventually, it will do this on its own, but to help it along, immediately add plantings close to, around, and right onto its walls. These vines, shrubs, and trees help ground the house to the land. Even a new mailbox needs this kind of attention. In the same way, a chaise longue placed in a room may look out of place at first as it is an ungainly but interesting piece of furniture. Try adding something to soften its presence, perhaps a reading lamp or a low magazine rack alongside it. At times all it takes is a small stack of strategically placed, well-read books to create a cozy, lived-in atmosphere. Be patient about this process. Know for certain that the end result will be just what you want it to be, and do not give up till you are totally satisfied.

There are a few carpets that will grace any room they enter. For the house I designed in Australia, exactly the right rugs presented themselves to me at the outset. As I was planning the living room, I found a large antique Agra with a soft maize ground and a Mogul pattern stenciled in deep gray, blue, and celadon, with touches of crimson. It was a breathtaking rug, probably one of the most beautiful I have ever found.

I rarely use Agras because they have a rather thick pile, and as a rule I prefer flat carpets. Thick rugs can swallow up the furniture placed on them like quicksand. But this particular Agra was a wonderful exception, light and lush and rich as Cornish cream, soft and smooth as silk velvet, and though not totally flat, quite lightweight in feeling, perhaps because of its age (see page 217). Its uncomplicated pattern and the luxurious quality of its weave made it a rare object of intense beauty. Surprisingly enough, it would cover a large portion of the room but not dominate it. We purchased the Agra on the spot. A trial run to Australia was not on the agenda, but in this case, it was not needed, because I had no doubt whatsoever that this exquisite piece would be perfect.

For the house's vast entryway, we found an eighteenth-century Aubusson to sit under and be protected by a circular center hall table. This rug is predominantly a pale caramel, with ivory, peach, and celadon tones woven into the intricate pattern. An early Bessarabian with caramel and maize hues on a mushroom-colored background was perfect for the family library, harmonizing brilliantly with the Agra in the living room and with the tones of the entry. All these carpets contained a common thread, a soft celadon color, so they worked well together, infusing the different spaces with a sense of connection. And for a study in another area of the house, we found another early Bessarabian, in mushroom, burnished red, and silvery tones.

The scale and formality of the house, which I have noted earlier, called for elaborate curtains and elegant fabrics. This was an interesting foray into a world I do not often get summoned to enter, and I enjoyed the opportunity to work with expanses of lush fabrics and piles of passementerie. It was a pleasure to be able to use color with a certain abandon. Here, working in a different context and country provided an unusually exciting experience for me. Variety brings vitality.

Every piece of furniture has
a personality, and it is
for us to determine if that
personality is compatible with
ours. This overscaled chair
in its original worn leather
sits in the corner of a
pool house pavilion.

Not every house needs many different floor coverings, but long expanses of floor can almost always benefit from the use of carpets. On the other hand, too many rugs can interrupt the flow of a well-waxed wood floor, and leave us feeling agitated. I have known some thick Oriental carpets to devour everything sitting upon them, beautiful people and extraordinary furniture alike. No matter how stunning or unusual it is, a carpet should not be the main focus of a room. Floors and rugs are, in essence, only part of the background of a room. It is not necessary to have a carpet jump out and greet us as we enter. It is far more seductive to be introduced slowly to the beauty at our feet.

You may find a marvelous rug that is much smaller than what you actually are looking for. If you are absolutely devoted to it, you will find a place for it. (This is a rule that you should apply to everything you own.) I will sometimes place a small rug under the coffee table as an accent instead of anchoring the furniture with a large one. It may not be exactly the perfect size for the room, but something slightly strange can make a space look less *designed* and give it personality. But please do not take this to extremes! Avoid bizarre affectations, or any self-conscious device that diverts attention from the beauty and comfort of the room as a whole.

You may prefer using a rug with an allover pattern, because those with center medallions can focus the space too rigidly and make the furniture placement somewhat difficult. Even so, you may come upon a rug with a center medallion that is just so lovely that you will have to adjust your plan to accommodate it. I am remembering a beautiful Bessarabian that had at its center the image of a bale of straw. It was simple yet enormously sophisticated, and it worked perfectly under a large, round, Georgian mahogany dining table.

An antique Bessarabian carpet in mushroom and magenta in a paneled library in Australia.

As you may have gathered, I am thoroughly biased in my carpet preferences. A deep-pile rug with a bold pattern is my least favorite option. High-piled carpets need to have a lawn mower run over them a few times to bring them down a bit. An especially beautiful Axminster or a brilliant Agra can make me relent on this, however. I actually prefer the back side to the front of many carpets, and although I admit I have never used a rug on its reverse, do not think it has not crossed my mind! I have used a seventeenth-century wall hanging on the floor of a bedroom—an area with very little traffic (see page 205). I have also used a tapestry with an allover pattern of leaves under a glass coffee table, where it is safe from spiky high heels.

Probably the most plentiful of the Persian carpets is the Tabriz. The Tabriz has a flatter weave than the lushly piled, velvety Agra. Early Tabrizes are far more interesting than the newer and more common ones, and since they do not always have a center medallion, they are also easier to work with. The Tabrizes I prefer are those made partially or entirely of cotton, though these excellent specimens are quite rare.

Karabaghs from the Caucasus are usually narrow runners or gallery-size rugs, with dark borders and geometric-type floral patterns that resemble those on Bessarabians. Often high in pile, they function well in hallways, where heavy traffic might otherwise devastate a flat-pile rug such as a Bessarabian.

Samarkands from East Turkestan often have quite vibrant colors. Usually narrow, they are what I term *decorative.* Their colors can be so brilliant that no more than one bright Samarkand runner can be used in a space, but several very muted Samarkands can work well together in a room.

The Amritsar carpets from the north of India are at their best when their design is clearly drawn and spaciously placed all over in patterns of spiraling vines (see page 197). Ziegler Sultanabad, from Persia, are famous for their luminous, light blue tones, which have no equal. An early Sultanabad may be flat and velvety with a wonderful overall pattern.

Among the European carpets are the flat-weave Bessarabians from the Ukraine featuring geometric floral patterns on a light field with darker borders. The eighteenth-century Bessarabians are European in feeling and lighter in color, but in the nineteenth century they became more Victorian than I would wish for. As with everything, there are exceptions.

The early needlework carpets from England and France can be glorious. The very good ones are delicate treasures, and are therefore difficult to use in areas that undergo much traffic. They are wonderful in a bedroom or small sitting room, or hung on museum walls.

Savonnerie, originally used to refer to the rugs woven in a disused soap factory in Paris, has now become a generic term for all hand-knotted carpets made in Spain, Belgium, and central Europe. They have a thick pile and, often, a large center medallion and lovely geometric shapes. I personally would prefer that they had a flatter weave.

Aubusson carpets from France do have a lovely flat weave, and the eighteenth-century examples can be incredibly beautiful. Some of the early Directoire Aubussons are masculine in tone and of fairly geometric design, which I like; they usually have a center medallion. Those of the Empire period are often too bold in color and somewhat coarse. As they graduate into their Louis Philippe period, they become too flowery and feminine for my taste. I would confine these designs to old, ritzy hotel powder rooms.

Axminster and Wilton rugs are classic English carpets. They are usually quite large and bold, with a thick, dense pile in bright pigments. They were winter carpets that were rolled up in the warmer months and exchanged for summer straw matting or perhaps cotton flat rugs. A good Axminister today is highly prized, and its price reflects its popularity. I have never been tempted to incorporate one into any project, because I find them too heavy and rather overpowering. If I do use one in the future, I suppose it would be for a paneled men's club, a private library, or a grand hall.

The Arts and Crafts rugs from England and Ireland are extremely interesting and are very popular today. I admire their clear colors and original designs. In modern projects I like to use Art Deco rugs, which are often cubist in design and look like abstract paintings. I especially love the ones with fresh, vivid colors. Older Navajo rugs can also look like abstract contemporary art in a room and they too are superb in modern settings.

Another type of rug that is a favorite of mine is the Polonaise. At one

The antique Agra carpet in this living room in Australia was the inspiration for the color palette of the entire room.

time they were incorrectly attributed to seventeenth- and eighteenth-century Polish factories; hence their names. We know now that they are Persian, though experts still differ on their exact place and date of origin. They are flat and worn and wonderful, and in a house I recently finished we used several. One that we used in a bedroom was predominately camel and green (see the photo on page 179). Polonaise rugs always have one long line of red in them—a quirky fact that I overlook. In the same house I used an early Kashgar that was woven with silver and burnished metal threads (see the photo on page 194).

There are definitely places where broadloom carpeting offers the most satisfactory solution. In a city apartment where noise is a factor, a good flat-weave carpet running from wall to wall is an excellent sound-proofing addition. Except in a very contemporary context, it is best to incorporate borders into all wall-to-wall carpets. A remark in a class-room lecture given by Michael Greer years ago has always stayed with me: "A carpet without a border is like a towel thrown into a room." An exception is when using straw or sisal carpets; designers tend to treat the matting itself as flooring. On stair runners try using a small border, even if it is just a twill tape. There are times, however, when the bronze or metal stair rods designed specifically for a project are all the decoration a dramatic winding staircase needs.

In a hallway, a solid broadloom carpet with a patterned border can define the space and add enormous charm to a sometimes forgotten area. I especially like patterned carpets and borders that have an uncut pile. They can have the delicate feeling of petit point. In city apartments, a wonderful way to make a small space appear larger is by carpeting the entire area, in the same way that painting all the walls the same color serves to create an unbroken flow. Carpeting can contain a space, soften its angles, and unify it in a way that no other floor covering can.

I once designed a projection room, which required carpeting to soften the noise. I covered the entire floor with a simple, flax-textured carpet in a palomino color and used a bright green, camel, and black Navajo rug under the coffee table, where it looked completely comfortable. If the floor had been made of wood, rather than carpeted, the small rug would have looked like a postage stamp floating on a sea of wooden boards; with the flat carpeting, however, it appeared as a piece of art rather than a rug. Smaller rugs can also be splendid when placed on sisal matting. My artistic photographer son Glen mentioned to me recently that one of his friends was using sisal matting in his apartment. When his friend asked him if he had ever seen it used anywhere before, Glen proudly declared, "But of course—my mom invented straw rugs." I thought the remark was very dear, yet it made me laugh. I had to explain to him that while perhaps *he* first saw straw in our house, sisal has been used for centuries and is still used by many today. In fact, the first straw floor coverings date to before 3000 B.C. in Egypt, and during the Middle Ages, the castles in northern Europe covered their floors in rush matting and dried grass. There is nothing new under the sun, especially not raffia or straw.

Dining rooms usually do best without any carpet whatsoever. I would rather dine on a clean, well-polished floor than on a spotted carpet. Besides, chairs seldom sit or move comfortably on most carpets.

Despite these realities, many prefer the quiet comfort of dining in a room with a rug. When using a rug under a table, make sure it is very flat so that chairs can move to and fro smoothly. The carpet should cover the area that the chairs will be pulled out to, and the walkway that forms the path for serving food should not be obstructed.

I recently completed a breakfast room in which I put a small, old

LEFT) A worn old American Indian cotton fabric hangs from an iron rod, creating a separate area in a small space. RIGHT) In my guest powder room a seventeenth-century English needlepoint mirror hangs over an antique wooden sink, which is truly a treasure.

stone chimney surround. The room looks out to a fanciful flower garden and has a balcony all its own. The floors are of the same wood as in the kitchen—a warm, light honey-colored walnut. But since it is near the main formal dining room and in constant use, I thought it should look less like a small room off the kitchen and more like an intimate country dining room.

Small rooms often take on a feeling of intimacy with the addition of a patterned carpet. After trying a myriad of flat rugs in the breakfast room, we settled happily on an extremely handsome multicolored straw mat. A year later, we found a wonderful, allover-patterned Bessarabian in an auction catalog and thought it too would look perfect in the breakfast room. Now the straw carpet is used during the summer months, and the patterned carpet is for the colder seasons. People often ask me to tell them what rug is right for a certain room, and I have to answer there are several choices, rarely just one. It is precisely the constant choices that make decorating so challenging. For this little breakfast room, there were three pleasing possibilities: absolutely nothing but the well-waxed wood floor; the round, straw mat; and the luscious patterned carpet—all were exactly right, yet each completely different.

The floor of an entry hall is a significant element in a house because entries are first impressions—once experienced, they are difficult to change. Most contain a minimal amount of furnishings: mirrors, side tables, a center hall table, or a bench seem to be all that is needed. Since the entry is the calling card for the rest of the house, it must be integrally planned to work with the rooms to which it leads.

The size of an entry is not very important. You may prefer to have a spacious living room rather than a large entry hall, yet you would do well to incorporate some space between the front door and the other rooms. It is disconcerting to walk into a living space without a proper entry; an entry is preferable, even if it is an area just large enough to turn around in.

In the country houses of Europe, entry halls can be quite elaborate, usually because they originally served the house in a variety of ways. Much of the estate and family business was once conducted in the entrance hall, so many contain fireplaces. I always use as many as I possibly can in a house, but thus far I have restrained myself from adding one to an entry. I like to think I may have that luxury one day.

Because the floor of an entrance hall is an element of consequence, it can feature a variety of materials: wood, stone, perhaps a mixture of the two, limestone, slate, marble and granite, stenciled wood, parquet, or tile, to name but a few. The material selected should create a harmonious transition from the outside of the house to the interior. There should be a sense of ease that flows into the adjoining hallways and rooms. An uncarpeted hard surface seems to do this best. The simplicity of old stone in an entry, with a few strong pieces of rustic furniture maybe even a solitary sculpture or a bench, can be a wonderfully welcoming introduction to almost any house.

In the photograph on page 200 of an entrance I recently completed in California, you can see an elaborate nineteenth-century marquetry French floor inlaid in many different woods. This floor was already in the house when it was purchased; it is said to have originally come from the château of the empress Joséphine and supposedly dates to when Napoléon Bonaparte was courting her. The table I found for that entry has documents to show that it once belonged to the sister of Bonaparte —simply a coincidence, since I did not choose it for this reason. I have laid a very old Japanese bamboo mat under the table in order to give the entry a less serious feel. The simplicity of that mat softens the floor's elaborate design.

A collection of English
comb-back chairs around a
sixteenth-century English
gateleg table.

One thing I have had to get accustomed to in Provence is the flooring typical to the region. It is rare to find wood floors—stone is used almost exclusively. The first floor of a house may have big slabs of beautiful uneven limestone, with marvelous crude, thick steps of the same ancient material. In both the farmer's house (the *mas*) and the gentleman farmer's house (the *bastide*), however, there are often terra-cotta tiles on the floors, frequently with many different shapes, butting into one another: squares, rectangles, octagons, and diamonds, all with different patterns and often of different colors and textures. While this is not easy to absorb into my design aesthetic, I am not as rigid as I would once have been.

I recently visited a small, exquisite château in the Dordogne that has terra-cotta tile floors in every room, several rooms with more than one type of tile. Because the tiles are so irregular and ancient, the floors are glorious. They give the rooms a great deal of their charm. If only new houses could look so comfortable with such eccentricities!

Objects of Desire

PRECEDING PAGE) **Books are the very best decoration, especially if you read them.** RIGHT) **This dining room was once too formal for its owner, and so I redesigned it to incorporate a pine library. Much less formidable, the room now feels more a part of the whole house.**

Unearthing an important—or, to anyone but yourself, an unimportant —treasure is enormously gratifying. Both my career and my flat in London have allowed me access to marvelous shops, private antiques dealers, auction houses, country house sales, and outdoor markets. The minute I step off the plane at Heathrow my energy level rises. On Wednesdays there is Camden Passage, and on Fridays at the crack of dawn I am off to Bermondsey, the large, outdoor market where a client of mine once found an Egon Schiele drawing for seventy pounds. On Saturdays there is the Portabello market, Westborne Grove, and again Camden Passage. And on Sundays there are always book fairs and antiques shows to attend. Charged and ready to work, I am inexhaustible.

When I was buying exclusively for Tarlow Antiques, I took frequent trips to Europe and had only a limited amount of time to spend in each country, so it was necessary to work fast. Scouring the markets with a

schedule in mind is superb training for the eye: you must see everything and very quickly. Most discerning dealers in antiques can go into a room full of furniture and objects and within seconds zoom in on what interests them. In my case this can sometimes be embarrassing—an associate may ask if I saw a certain piece of furniture that was on view at an auction house I visited that very day, and I'll have no idea what he is talking about. It was not in my line of vision.

People who collect out of love are exempt from the dictates that govern traditional design, for there are no rules for true lovers. Passionate collectors often give their houses an enchanted quality. Then there are those who end up with overwhelming clutter or with cold, museum-like displays. Finally, the difference is in how people relate to their treasures. Quality, not quantity, is what makes collections captivating.

In completing a room, we depend on the accessories to give it character. The most intimate and interesting parts of a room are its objects—especially the pieces that have a charm of their own and reflect the identity of the person who treasures them. A piece of porcelain, a small, beautifully woven basket, a smooth stone found on some faraway shore—these evoke memories and meld the past with the present. Our prized possessions are keys to our personalities, and what interests us is usually the most interesting thing about us.

Perhaps the most wonderful accessory comes in the form you now hold in your hands—a book. When I look back to the rooms I have been most enchanted by, they were invariably ones with walls that were lined with books. Like windows, bookshelves can add depth to a room in ways that paintings and wall hangings rarely do. If I were forced to choose, I would much prefer to live surrounded by carefully selected and much loved books than by indifferent art.

I remember an intimate dinner party in a small room where the walls were entirely lined with books. They were on shelves that a designer had built and lacquered a very black brown. The shelves were narrow, so as not to impose themselves on the small room, and filled with books of every color and size. Large art books rested sideways, others stood upright, and the effect was an intriguing and colorful geometry of horizontal and vertical shapes. No other objects were placed on the shelves—only books, crammed together in a totally arresting way.

We dined at a glass table that doubled as a desk during the day. The floor of the room was covered with a flat, woven geometric deco rug in which one of the predominant colors was a rich brick red. The chairs were old and of natural wicker. Our host used an odd mix of brilliant gem-colored glassware that glowed in the candlelight and made a subtle connection with the colorful books on the shelves.

I thought of that intimate room years later, when a client was concerned that his formal dining room was too grand in feeling and too large in scale for his bachelor lifestyle. We transformed the imposing space into a pine-paneled library–dining room that proved very much in keeping with his Georgian-style house and with the other pine-paneled rooms of the first floor (see the following page).

When I first saw this house it felt totally disconnected; every room had a separate point of view, and the molding in each of the main rooms was different. The challenge was to simplify and contain the variety. Adding even more pine paneling, like any continuous, recurring element in a design, served to unite the entire floor plan.

When we paneled the dining room and redesigned the moldings, we created a setting that was infinitely more harmonious. Using bookshelves of the same pale pine made the entire space smaller in scale and far more inviting. With the shelves filled with books, art, and artifacts, a

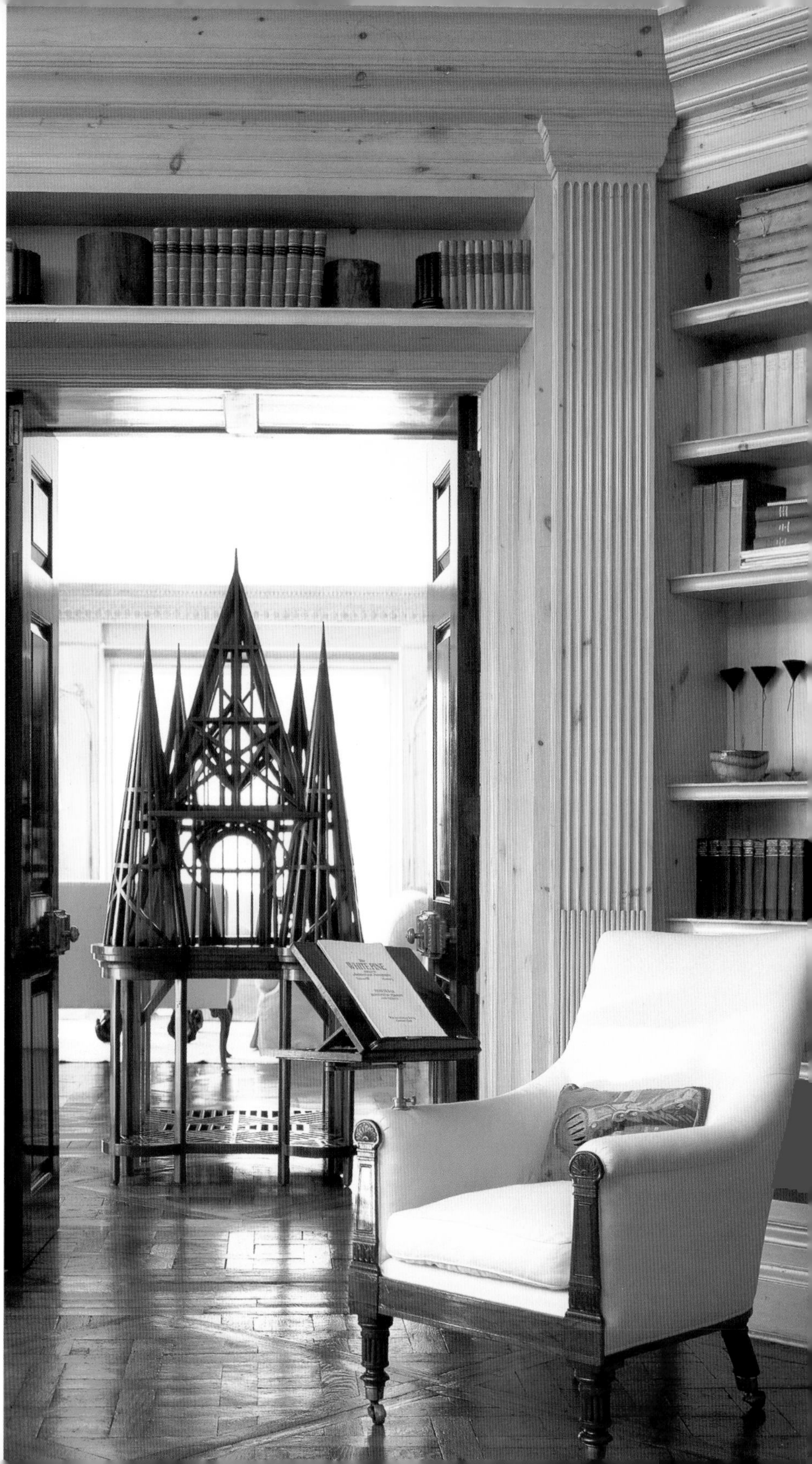

A corner of a library–dining
room has an unusual English
chair with its own reading
stand.

cold, formal dining room became a warm, elegant space and a central
element in the house.

Another memorable book-lined room was the bedroom of my friend
Ralph Webb, a gifted fabric and furniture designer. This glorious square
room was furnished for two with twin queen-sized four-poster beds
that faced each other from opposite walls. White lawn fabric hung from
the beds' wooden poles, falling simply onto the floor. The walls were
completely covered from top to bottom with bookshelves, and more
books were stacked in piles on the floor near the beds. Other than the
books and the views from the uncurtained windows, there was very little adornment in the room. Books, air, light—I cannot imagine a better
room in which to rest.

Bookshelves are like doors and windows in that their dimension and
placement demand the most serious consideration. I often use them as
architectural elements, but bookshelves do not have to be built in; the

freestanding brass shelves Billy Baldwin designed for Cole Porter's study are timeless. Among other materials, I have used very thin steel tubing to create Erector-set type shelving. I like the freshness they contribute.

Balance was once fundamental to what most architects and designers considered a correct room. Today, unfortunately, windows and doors are not always built on-axis, their size and shape can have questionable relationships, and placement can be haphazard. When I remodel a room I often rely on bookshelves to correct such architectural problems, and they can aid greatly in camouflaging a poorly balanced space. In their design and dimensions, bookshelves can also raise the height of a room. When windows and doors do not relate sympathetically, I consider building in shelves as the space's unifying element, even to the point of extending them over the doorways.

This Georgian library ladder is extremely architectural, with an almost Oriental simplicity about it. Its very presence quite comfortably and confidently interrupts the continuous flow of bookshelves.

I collect books on architecture, art, and literature, and while some are rare editions, all are on subjects I am passionate about. I keep many of these books in my living room. Placed on their shelves, they become a canvas against which I display drawings, sculptures, and special objects.

My bookshelves display artifacts alongside treasures I have culled from construction sites—modern sculpture at its most uncomplicated. During the building of the Getty Center, I would comb the construction site with its architect. He was looking for objects to build large sculptures with; I was interested in small pieces that were sculptures in their own right—a stone or a piece of metal with a special shape, patina, or color. These found treasures are my Giacomettis, my Brancusis. I am not recommending that everyone dig through construction or dump sites for their accessories. I am just suggesting that we not be afraid to display any simple, interesting object. My only rule is that nothing adorn my life that is not precious to me. I must respect its shape, color, meaning, and quality. An object added for effect instead of affection will always look like an affectation.

Whenever I decide to add to or replace the objects on my shelves, it takes up an inordinate amount of time to rearrange them. During the process, I imagine myself as an artist painting a picture, transforming one shelf at a time slowly and earnestly. When I am finished I first look at the whole picture, at all the shelves in context with the room, and then at each shelf as it relates to the others. With this perspective, I try to notice colors or shapes that may be distracting from the balance of the whole. If the arrangement is too harmonious, too static, or too conventional, I edit or make the changes that will bring life to my picture. I go back and study the work in progress again and again. For me, editing is one of the most important elements of any design process.

In my London flat, books are the featured players on my shelves, in all colors, shapes, and sizes. I allow very few objects to intrude upon them. A pair of antique Queen Anne mirrors hang on either side of the fireplace. I have searched for a pair of cabinets to put under the mirrors in order to ground them to the floor, but until I find exactly the right ones, I will continue to use stacks and stacks of *Country Life* magazines piled high below them.

In the same room, the television sits on a bronze gueridon, looking quite pleased with itself simply because it has been allowed to be seen. It, too, is piled high with books. I do not usually display any sort of media paraphernalia, and have even been known to tuck telephones away in old wooden boxes. Yet in this case the room is so imposing in scale and content that I wanted to bring it down a peg; the modern television set gives the room an authentic lived-in quality.

To ensure that your books contribute to that cozy quality, collect only subjects you care about and continually search for more books on those subjects. Visit bookshops and book fairs, and keep up with library sales at auction. Book loving cannot be simulated; bookshelves filled with magazines and auction catalogs can be far more interesting than rows of expensive leather-tooled books bought by the yard. We may not be able to tell a book by its cover, yet we can often tell quite a bit about people's personalities by the books they own. Though no one likes the expression *coffee-table book,* a stack of well-chosen, beautifully illustrated volumes on a table can uniquely express the passions of the person to whom they belong. (It is disappointing, however, to discover that the books have never been opened, or that they are on subjects that seem totally outside the owner's interests.)

As with books, art is one of the most subjective and personal choices we can make in our house. In fact, the art we display can only make a more personal statement if we create it ourselves. Many of us are left

LEFT) In a guest powder room for gentlemen, a Chinese altar table holds a bronze bowl as its sink. Sliding Japanese doors cover the mirror that reflects a Japanese screen on the opposite wall. RIGHT) The Japanese paper screen of fish swimming upstream adorns a wall in the gentlemen's powder room. There is also a ladies' gossip room right next door.

cold by collecting that has its roots in acquisition rather than in passionate appreciation. Purchasing art for its future value is almost like framing stocks or bonds. This is why I try not to become involved in my clients' purchases of pictures or sculpture, and acquire work only for my own pleasure.

Just recently I completed a house for a collector who owns some truly wonderful works of art. Although the client has relied on me for many aspects of the design of the house, I have not participated in selecting his constantly growing and changing collection. As is the case with many art collections, the works move around, sometimes within the house and sometimes on loan to museums. Whenever I design for art collectors, I try not to anticipate where any of the pieces will eventually hang, because I want the client to be free to move the collection about the house. Rooms are therefore designed to stand by themselves, with the knowledge that art would sometimes grace their walls. Nothing competes with the art; my goal is always to create a house that subtly envelops a collection and offers multiple options for its display.

The juxtaposition of contemporary pieces with antiques makes a room young and alive. Although I have been identified with my passion for antiques, I refrain from using too many of them in one place, for I learned long ago that too many pieces of antique furniture and accessories in one room can be oppressive. In the same way, a house that is very modern needs contrasts, some objects of a different period to enhance its beauty and soften its lines. We should not attempt to create museums, but rather should strive for comfortable living spaces of character and beauty.

Approach any house not as a series of separate decisions but as a multilayered process. Challenged by the space, first think about what you wish the final outcome to be, and then begin to work on the particulars. Start with the architectural changes that will be required or, in the case of a house that does not yet exist, with the blueprints for construction. Continue with the floor plans and furniture placement, then fill in your drawing with color schemes and fabric selections; consider what you need to purchase and how you will edit what you already have. Close your eyes and see everything that you have chosen in place. Perhaps your picture is not exactly how it will look when the house is finished, but anticipate that this image will not be too far from actuality.

Once you have your house somewhat in order, now comes the time to start living in it. Share it with your world. Although it may seem important to wait until every last detail is in place before inviting guests in, do not procrastinate—plan a party. I have found that this is an excellent way bring in life and to feel at home in your new house.

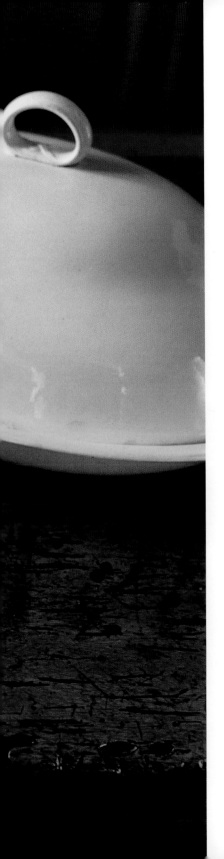

Open House

PRECEDING PAGE) Ivory-handled
bread knives next to a Leeds-
ware covered platter. RIGHT)
It took me years to find an
authentic lazy Susan. Collecting old serving treasures takes
entertaining to another level.

2 4 4

When I first entertained as a young woman, any event, large or small, was an anxiety-ridden ordeal. I always felt that my family and friends expected something extraordinary from me. The pressure I experienced was enormous, although it was a burden I inflicted upon myself. Looking back, I am quite sure that the finicky and fancy meals I presented to my guests made them wish they had stayed at home. And it was always the same: no matter how prepared I thought I was, at the last minute I inevitably lacked the proper serving pieces, the right platter, or the necessary number of dessert plates, and I would find myself exhausting all my energy and enthusiasm in searching for them. As a consequence, being a hostess became a chore, and not surprisingly I had no interest in entertaining: I had denied myself the pleasure of enjoying my guests.

I have learned that the more you entertain, the easier it becomes. If you are well prepared and you entertain frequently—and frequency is the key—these occasions become delightful variations on a familiar

ABOVE) Grasses bring freshness indoors in a way plants seldom do. LEFT) These wonderful serving pieces were once old dented copper objects that I transformed by silvering them. The dents remain so the feeling of age is not lost.

theme. So I make it a habit to entertain, even if I invite only one extra person at a time. The preparation has become progressively easier as my circle of guests has expanded. I no longer feel that I must surpass everyone's expectations, especially my own.

When I am in London I like to serve cozy dinners by the fire in cool weather; during the summer, I entertain on the garden terrace. Londoners love to dine in the garden, and in the summer months there it stays light until ten in the evening. These are wonderful evenings, but when I am working constantly, especially after long country jaunts buying antiques, I tend to resist the idea of inviting friends over. I am always pleased when I transcend my inclination to stay home with a book at the end of a heavily scheduled day. Once I have decided to entertain, the planning and presentation can become fun and creative. You can create a small dining area just about anywhere you choose. A little gateleg table can be opened to serve two. It may not be as roomy and comfortable as a large table in the dining room, but it is the very essence of intimacy to share a meal with a friend or a loved one at a very small table. Whomever you include as your dining partner—date, mate, child, or friend—he or she will feel especially privileged.

What is important is how relaxed you are. This matter of ease can be elusive. A designer friend, Leonard Stanley, lives in a truly wonderful house and has enormous personal style. On the occasions when I have been invited to visit, his treasures and his charmingly elegant way of entertaining have delighted me. I remember a dinner in his garden one glorious California summer evening. An antique table had been set outside under a willowy flowering tree. A remarkable cut-crystal chandelier was hanging from the bough of one of its branches, glowing in the night, entirely lit with candles. It was a dazzling experience, the kind that lingers in my memory of enchanted moments. It had taken him days to prepare for this small dinner party, which is why he rarely entertains—he put so much effort into his splendid evening that it could not be repeated frequently. I would rather not make entertaining quite so daunting.

I have found that only a sense of relaxed routine makes entertaining a joy. Make sure that everything in your house is always waxed, scrubbed, and sparkling, so that you are comfortable having friends drop by. I am usually busy at my work, so I am not involved in the day-to-day details of cleaning and maintaining the house. But there are times when I have an overwhelming need to care for it myself, even if it is just to go through all the cupboards and rearrange the linen closet. Focusing on this mundane activity gives me enormous pleasure, in much the same way, I am sure, that tending a garden does to someone who loves to work outdoors. When I put the simple things in order, I renew my deep

PRECEDING PAGE) **A pine plate rack holds an array of pewter chargers and a collection of Dutch bottles.** RIGHT) **A cozy dining room.**

connection with the house; I enjoy the intimate experience of tending to it physically.

Certain touches can make me feel especially relaxed about welcoming guests. Years ago, if I did not have fresh flowers in the house I would not allow anyone in the door. Now I usually do have fresh flowers, but I have also discovered that growing pots full of green grasses means there is always something alive and fresh. And grasses do not need to be replaced as often as flowers do!

One of the other things that makes serving guests easier these days is that I actually have the right serving pieces. Once I never had what I needed when I needed it. At this point in my life, I experience the opposite: I have such a wide and varied collection of unusual serving pieces that I could open a shop. Searching in shops and antiques markets all over the world, I have gathered linens, creamware, porcelain, flatware, china, and other special pieces that make serving guests a joyful experience.

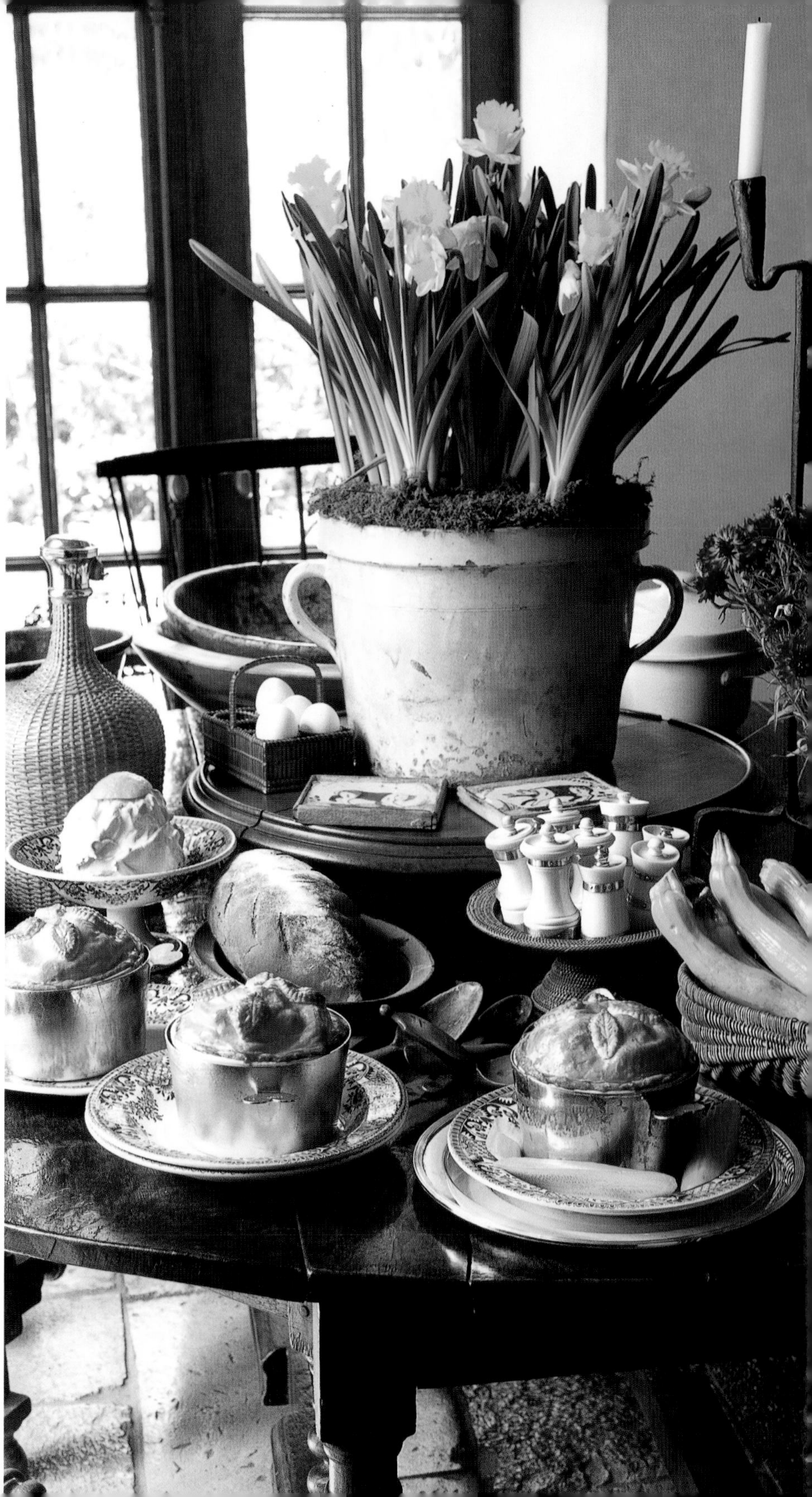

**Buffets present myriad
opportunities to share not only
your culinary skills, but your
creative artistry as well.**

   And I find almost as much pleasure in looking for these things as I do in using them. On my last trip to England, I found an unusual wooden-handled serving spoon, with the spoon part formed out of dented old copper. I silver-plated the copper, leaving the dents as they were, waxed the crude wood handle, and what emerged was a beautiful object. I have also silver-plated some big, old copper pots, and they are just the right size for buffet-style serving. Again, I left the dents intact, and they look splendid on the English gateleg table upon which I lay out a buffet in my kitchen. Another example is a cracked creamware vegetable dish with its ancient repair staples showing. My posh English antiques dealer friends tease me for scouting out such eccentric or distressed items. With their auction-room pallor, they express amazement when I brave freezing weather in an outdoors antiques market at some ungodly hour in the morning to find a bit of early crockery. But the beauty of these objects never ceases to dazzle them when they later dine at my table.

In Europe, mealtime is sacrosanct. In Paris at the Marché aux Puces, even during the freezing cold days of midwinter, when lunchtime arrives a rope is tied neatly across each antiques booth to keep shoppers from entering. A table is then set up in the middle of the space, sometimes covered with a lovely old cloth. And then they sit, the French dealers, their friends, and their families, sharing several bottles of wine over a generous and lengthy lunch. You could offer to buy their entire stock of furniture and they would pretend that you did not exist. At that moment in time, nothing is more important to them than the quality of their noonday repast.

Sharing an intimate time with friends over a delicious meal can add tremendously to the quality of life. Where the meal is held or what is on its menu are not nearly as important as how relaxing the atmosphere is. Unless you are an inspired chef, develop a repertoire of simple dishes to serve, adding a few new ones every few years and ignoring an old specialty for a while. For a winter buffet, I will put an osso buco on the table in one of my deep kettles. Beside it is a large antique pottery dish that will hold the spaetzle; there will be a creamware bowl for some vegetables; a large wood trough for the salad; and a delicately woven basket to hold the popovers. (I serve sumptuous popovers because they are easy to make, taste delicious, and, best of all, look divine on the buffet table.) The guests move from the living room through the dining room, find their seats, and continue on to the kitchen to gather their dinner.

Try using well-worn accessories, different in material and character; mixing important objects with simple, precious, primitive pieces can become part of your personal style. Serving a buffet in the winter at a table set with these special objects allows you to create a Dutch still life. Whether or not you are entertaining, consider using your best things on an everyday basis. Even when my children were very young I did not allow paper napkins in the house. If things are considered too valuable to use every day, then what value do they have to our actual lives?

My house is arranged so that it can be as intimate with a large number of guests as it is for small dinners. I can seat twelve people in the dining room without extending the refectory table, or sixteen with it open, and I have an old country walnut table in storage that seats twenty-two. If I need more seating, I have two tables in the kitchen that will each seat ten. The lighting, the food, and the general sense of ease turn a large dinner party into a warm, intimate evening.

On one occasion, the guests gathered in the living room for the first course, a handsome slab of smoked sturgeon served from my old silver-and-mahogany trolley, with a basket of brown bread and a bowl of horseradish sauce. Then we left the high-ceilinged living room, with its tall vases filled with branches of forsythia and its two lit fireplaces radiating a special smoky scent, and entered the lower, cozier, wood-beamed dining room. There, the long country pearwood table was set with white linen napkins so large that when you put them in your lap they almost touched the ground. There were daffodils on the sideboard, and the flickering candles in the chandelier were reflected in the domed silver covers at every place setting. Lifting the domes, each guest found the second course—a hot, crusty pot pie.

When the kitchen is used for seating, it is important that all the food preparation be completed before the guests enter the room for dinner. This is why the appetizer was served in the living room and the second course was already on the table when they entered the kitchen. When the silver lids that covered the entrée were removed, the pies were still piping hot, and the accompanying salad, breads, and cheeses could be easily served once people were seated. Though silver domes with ivory handles might seem pretentious in a formal dining room, in this rustic kitchen setting they were charming. Once again, the juxtaposition of the crude with the elegant was delightful. Whenever I entertain, I count on the house to work its magic every bit as much as the food, the drink, and the vibrant personalities of my friends.

Simple, scrumptious, unpretentious food, served with ease, lies at the heart of some of the best experiences I can remember. Besides my mother, the hostesses I learned most from are two American women living in London. I became acquainted with both twenty years ago, just a few years before I bought my London flat. It was a good time for them to enter my life, for I was able to absorb their very particular styles.

The first hostess introduced me to the secret of relaxing and enjoying

The sensuality of old wood is evident in the primitive quality of these spoons. The tiles, the oldest I have ever seen, are actually small works of art.

my own entertaining. She never made her guests feel as if they were guests, just cozy friends sharing an intimate meal. I think what made us feel so welcomed was how completely relaxed and comfortable she was in her home. I have seen my friend move with her family from a house on Chester Square in London to a temporary mews house on Eaton Square, and then to a house in Los Angeles, and she always takes her remarkable ease at entertaining with her. With or without the help of her writer husband, she will manage to prepare a superb dinner with little assistance and great style. Meals hosted by this couple mean outstanding food simply served, without apparent effort exerted in any way. And no matter where their household is at that moment, you can always be sure of dining with a fascinating mix of people.

My friend Marguerite Littman is an American southerner, and dinner or lunch at her table is perhaps the most sought-after invitation in London. This hostess exemplifies the southern hospitality that enchants even the English. Foremost, the menu is something to look forward to. Even if the guests were dull, which they never are, you would still dine and drink with pleasure. Marguerite has a fair repertoire of different dishes, but over the years you are bound to find a certain recipe repeated several times. I have come to appreciate and even to look forward to this; in fact, I often feel alarmed if something new is being served—that is, until I take the first bite. Whatever the menu—perhaps her summer favorite of mango and cold lobster, or filet of sole with honey-baked bananas—there is always a delicious play of taste and texture.

Marguerite and her husband, Mark, like to have their guests for lunch, sometimes on Saturdays but more usually during the week. I once asked why and was told it was because this way there was a beginning and an end, meaning that at the close of the meal everybody returns to the business of living. They also favor inviting members of couples separately; they never neglect either partner, for if they ask one to lunch today, the other will be invited soon after. Their rationale is that this way the individuals do not restrict each other, and you can experience the best of each. Louis XV and Madame de Pompadour followed the same practice, giving their guests unlimited license to be an individual and not part of a pair.

At a typical lunch, we first gather in the living room for a light drink; in the summer it could be Bellinis, with fresh peach juice and Champagne. No hors d'oeuvres are served—ever. After drinks we have a superb lunch in the dining room, always with good conversation, then espresso, and then everyone leaves, utterly content. For many years the dining room was decorated seamlessly with a bright red floral fantasy fabric, which was both charming and flattering, even on a foggy, London afternoon. At this moment the decor is somewhat less dramatic, with a subtle light-colored stripe, but the chandelier and the table and chairs are still the same, which is comforting. None of us likes too much change in the rooms we have come to love.

Marguerite's guests are always stimulating conversationalists. The small group might include museum people, diplomats, politicians, or artists. And there is always an intriguing combination of guests: a bright college student who is visiting from abroad might be seated next to a Hollywood mogul or a cabinet minister.

You might conclude that these parties are brilliant because many of the guests are of such distinction. But distinguished guests are no guarantee of a pleasant event. Celebrities do not always mix well, as I learned years ago to my dismay. The first party I ever gave in my California house was not a great success, as I was under the delusion that the more accomplished the people you invite, the better the party. Big mistake! Most celebrities like to be the center of attention, and if they are not, they may not play well with the others. My second mistake that evening was that I served tiny squab: the dish I thought would be so unusual turned out to resemble a meal of plucked canaries! The lessons I learned that night were that too many stars do not make a sparkling night, and that we should offer guests only what we would normally serve ourselves—simple fare. The effort of trying to impress always leaves me feeling *de*pressed. Even the word *trying* makes me anxious.

Gene Hovis, a New York cookbook author and brilliant host, serves his guests homey comfort food, huge casseroles of delicious macaroni and cheese and a perfect glazed ham. Bill Blass, probably the most elegant man on earth, is famous for his special meatloaf and red-pepper jelly. Connie Wald, a California hostess whom everybody loves to visit, will serve a delicious platter of fried chicken or a huge plate of penne

In a corner of a guest bedroom reside a pair of antique wing chairs still covered in their original leather. A rare English comb-back rocker is placed to enjoy the fire on cold winter days.

with vodka tomato sauce to the most special guest list you can imagine. What takes these hosts and hostesses out of the ordinary is how they present their simple dinners.

Serving with confidence does mean careful preparation. Set the table beforehand and choose the music you want to hear that evening; let it begin playing. Then come through the entryway as if you were a guest. Move through the living room and the dining room, leaving the kitchen for later. Pay attention to your guests' experience. Passing one of the sofas, I may notice that if four people should sit down together, someone will be left without a pillow at their back. I add a few. I look in at the powder room—are there enough linen towels and a few flowers?

Tonight the flowers in the living room are masses of white tuberoses, standing gracefully in two tall glass bowls. On another evening I may use yellow forsythia, which looks lovely in the spring, especially when I open the doors to the dining room and you can see a profusion of yellow daffodils on the sideboard. Still another time I might use tall, cream-colored French tulips, huge white dahlias, or white dogwood and lovely bright green grasses. Whatever flowers I select, I have only one kind in each room, and sometimes only one kind throughout the house, depending on what is available that season. And be careful not to set out too many flowers—a house should appear natural and relaxed, not over-dressed for a party.

I look over the drinks tray, making sure to put in place everything needed in the way of beverages. I have a collection of small trays for serving drinks, including a flat Indian basket that can hold as many as four glasses safely. I lay fresh linen cloths in each tray. If I am having someone serve the drinks, I make sure they have everything they need to work with. Out comes an old serving trolley to be set with a silver-and-ivory coffee service, demitasse cups, napkins, chocolates, and a wonderful wooden box of cigars; then it is rolled away until after dinner. A tray of silver and crystal after-dinner liqueur decanters is prepared; this, too, will be carried out to the living room while we are dining. I have, stacked away, a set of small, very light 1920 steel-and-cream leather chairs that offer a refreshing contrast to the antique pieces in my house; they will be brought out while we are dining and placed around the fireplaces, so that after dinner small groups of guests can gather and talk as they have their coffee and cognac.

You may find that if a group of guests is larger than ten, they will not want to sit before dinner; they will prefer to stand, conversing and holding their drinks. If no one is on hand to serve drinks, you may choose to set a tray of glasses on a table in the living room so that the guests can help themselves. Next to the wine glasses I place a small, neat basket filled with linen napkins. With drinks comes the appetizer, and I serve only one. I find that passing different plates of hors d'oeuvres is too formal and detracts from the relaxed atmosphere.

One of my favorite dinners for a group of twelve people or fewer is Chinese fare. I start with crisp, freshly made little spring rolls or fried dumplings on a long, flat, wooden baguette tray. I have served this appetizer for many different dinners and often for the same guests. When something is as delicious as these are, you can continue to have it again and again.

I like serving a Chinese dinner because it allows me to use my collection of Chinese treasures. After the spring rolls, served in the living room, we sit down at the table for hot soup or steamed dumplings, served in the ancient Sung bowls that often adorn my living room bookshelves. The table is laid with white linen placemats and napkins and set with flat celadon dishes, Victorian amethyst wine glasses, and silver water goblets; the combination of the muddy celadon with the pur-

LEFT) A seventeenth-century French cabinet. When I built my kitchen, I designed it around this exceptionally large cabinet. BELOW) This trolley is sometimes wheeled from the dining room into the living room to serve the first course there.

ple and the silver is ravishing. Each place has its own set of antique chopsticks in individual cases of tortoise, shagreen, cloisonné, and jade. Once everything is in place, I can relax for the rest of the evening. If I am having a fantastic time, I am confident that everyone else is too.

Entertaining can bring pleasure and creativity to your life, and even a large-scale event can be infused with warmth and ease, though the preparation will be far more daunting. Both the challenges and the rewards of formal entertaining were present when I gave my friend Richard a birthday party in a Malibu Beach house he had designed. His clients were friends who kindly contributed the house for the occasion and were the co-hosts of the party. I had thrown big birthday parties before, but since this was a special birthday, I wanted it to be celebrated in a house that he had designed. We invited a hundred people, and it was such a beautiful warm evening in October that we did not need a tent, though we had a backup strategy in the event that it rained. The preparations were elaborate: the tennis court, where dinner would be served, was completely enclosed with tall hedges. I had a sixty-foot table running the length of the area, with over a thousand square votive candles flickering, so that the table was ablaze with light. So too was the house —tall, white, and spectacular, a shimmering star on this gloriously starlit night. Drinks were served in the living room and on the terrace overlooking the ocean. The men marched around like proud penguins in their tuxedos, and the women were stunning in their elegant party dresses. An orchestra played on the terrace, and the entire scene was unbelievably ravishing.

   Seating everyone was the most difficult part: one or two guests had to cancel at the last minute, and rearranging the places at the long table was a demanding feat. When we were seated, I looked with immense pleasure and satisfaction down the table as the faces of our friends glowed in the flickering candlelight. Friends and family talk of this party to this day, recalling the long, lovely table and the ten waiters who carried in ten white birthday cakes shaped like architectural elements, all covered in sparklers. It was magical.

Three years after that party we gave another one, at the same house. This time we were celebrating the opening of the Getty Center with a party for three hundred people in a tent on the tennis court. It was mid-December, a week before Christmas, so we expected it to be cold. For months before, we were preparing the house, listening to bands, tasting food, designing invitations, looking at lighting, and taking care of a multitude of other details.

The tent had been filled with very large pine trees; I wanted it to feel

A large country kitchen gives
every opportunity to indulge
one's fantasies of rural life.

as if we were not in a tent in Malibu but in the thick of a forest. The trees were shimmering with tiny white lights. After we tested the lighting, everyone went home to await the party the next evening.

What we had not anticipated was a minor hurricane with torrential rains. By morning half the pine trees had floated off to sea. Rain and wind had raged all night, the tent had collapsed; everything was ruined. But the tent was resurrected and repaired. The trees that had not washed out to sea were restored to their original positions inside the tent. Dozens of new trees were brought in to replace those that had drifted out to the ocean. When the guests entered the tent, tiny snowflakes, which were actually created by a trick of lighting, covered the room. After a minute or two the snow subsided and there appeared a winter wonderland. It was, after all, the most perfect party ever.

This painted dugout chair is part of my collection, and a rare piece of sculpture in its own right. We use the old badminton rackets constantly with real feathered birds that are increasingly difficult to find.

ACKNOWLEDGMENTS In any creative endeavor there are always many minds and talents at work. I'd like to give special thanks to my agent, Lynn Nesbit, for her constant encouragement, and for believing in *The Private House* so enthusiastically. Thanks also go to my excellent, patient, and perfectionist editor, Annetta Hanna; to art director Marysarah Quinn, whose talent and incredible eye helped create a book worth looking at; and to designer Richard Ferretti for adding his special magic. Many thanks to Jane Treuhaft, Camille Smith, and Liz Royles at Clarkson Potter for their valuable contributions. Last but not least, I am grateful to my dear friends at Melrose House, whose stability and support are truly gifts to treasure.

ABOUT THE AUTHOR Rose Tarlow is a nationally recognized antiquaire, furniture and fabric designer, and interior designer whose work has been featured in many publications, including *Architectural Digest, The New Yorker, Town & Country, House Beautiful,* the *New York Times, House & Garden, Elle Décor, W Magazine, Veranda, Interior Design, Casa Vogue,* the *London Telegraph,* and the *Los Angeles Times.* Her company, Rose Tarlow–Melrose House, is based in Los Angeles. Her furniture and fabrics are featured in fourteen additional satellite locations throughout the country. When her schedule allows, Ms. Tarlow teaches a master class at UCLA's School of Interior Design; this book is a personal summary of what she teaches in her class.